A BOX

of

DARKNESS

Also by Sally Ryder Brady

Instar

A Yankee Christmas: Featuring Nantucket

A Yankee Christmas: Featuring Vermont

Sweet Memories
(with Sara Pinto, Sarah Underwood, and Lucia Frigerio)

A BOX

of

DARKNESS

The Story of a Marriage

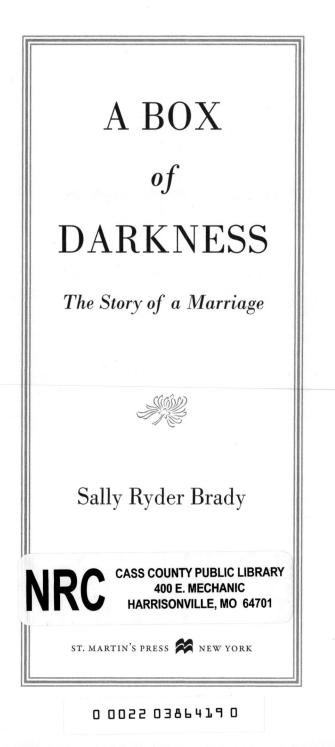

Sally Ryder Brady

ST. MARTIN'S PRESS NEW YORK

"This Paper Boat" reprinted from *Valentines* by Ted Kooser by permission of the University of Nebraska Press. Copyright © 1996, 2006 by Ted Kooser. Copyright © 2008 by the Board of Regents of the University of Nebraska.

"The Uses of Sorrow" reprinted from *Thirst* by Mary Oliver. Copyright © 2006 by Mary Oliver. Published by Beacon Press, 2006.

www.stmartins.com

Design by Meryl Sussman Levavi

Library of Congress Cataloging-in-Publication Data

Brady, Sally Ryder.
    A box of darkness : the story of a marriage / Sally Ryder Brady. — 1st ed.
        p. cm.
    ISBN 978-0-312-65416-0
    1. Brady, Sally Ryder—Marriage.   2. Authors, American—20th century—Family relationships.   3. Husbands—Death—Psychological aspects.   I. Title.
    PS3552.R244Z46 2011
    813'.54—dc22
    [B]
                                                                2010039416

First Edition: February 2011

10 9 8 7 6 5 4 3 2 1

For Upton

AUTHOR'S NOTE

This is a true story, though some names have been changed.

ACKNOWLEDGMENTS

Writers, when they are writing, are often needy creatures. But to write in the immediate void left by the death of my partner for life rendered me needy in brand-new ways. Without the patient and very generous attention of family and friends, I could not have navigated the unknown, dark waters of grief as I did in the year of writing *A Box of Darkness*.

My four admirable children, Sarah Brady Underwood, Andrew Upton Birnie Brady, Nathaniel Francis Ryder Brady, and Alexander Childs Brady, supported me in ways as various as the supporters themselves, taking time out of their busy lives to listen to me, to ease my financial burden while I wrote the book, to provide me with some of the liveliest anecdotes, and to keep me from exaggerating the story, or slipping into maudlin self-pity or repellent rage. *A Box of Darkness* comes with their collective and individual blessings.

Joan Ryder Wickersham, my sister and my most devoted and energetic fan, gave me a bright room overlooking Vineyard Sound in which to write, peaceful days, and evenings of good company and good food. She also eagerly followed the ripening story almost chapter by chapter, never letting her praise or enthusiasm flag.

Most of the book was written in the cottage belonging to my friend Kitty Bacon. Kitty is certainly the fairy godmother of this book and maybe my fairy godmother as well. With her own keen writer's eye, she tirelessly and astutely read every draft, offered insightful feedback, and refilled my glass of Prosecco.

William Craig, verbal acrobat and wizard, leads the pack of sharp-eyed readers. His polish glows on every page, but his kindness and compassion were also crucial to me as I stumbled through thorny passages. Marion Brady, Tracy Brady, Samm Carlton, Glynn Christian, Sylvia Davatz, Erika Goldman, Sophia Healy, Sasha Helper, Abigail Holstein, Laurie Horowitz, Cynthia Linkas, Andrés Lorente, Christina Lynch, Deborah Luquer, Patty Patterson, Barbara Raives, Judy Richardson, Nina Ryan, Lucy Talbott, Miriam Weinstein, and Bert Wickersham all helped to shape the book through their attentive reading and wise comments, and I am very grateful to each of them. I thank Kathryn Lasky for helping to spread the word, Anita Keefe for many warm welcomes, Philip White for quiet help, and Wayan Buschman for her green pencil.

Special thanks to Bruce Kennett for his early design of the beautiful jacket, and for all his help with the selection and placement of photographs, and their surrounding text.

Sue Quinn not only read the book but recommended it to her splendid agent, Jill Kneerim, who is now my agent, a great stroke of good fortune for me. Jill and her savvy assistant, Caroline Zimmerman, continue to skillfully shepherd this book, while sowing and watering seeds for books to come.

I am blessed to have had quicksilver Charlie Spicer to edit and champion my book, and tireless, efficient, and cheerful Allison Strobel to take care of myriad, perplexing details. The extraordinary combination of professional skill and rampant personal enthusiasm I've experienced throughout St. Martin's Press was sparked, I suspect, by publisher Sally Richardson together with Charlie, and for this, too, I feel incredibly lucky.

For these past two stormy years, I have been fed physically and psychically by so many of you, and if I haven't mentioned you by name, I trust you to recognize yourself and accept my thanks.

THIS PAPER BOAT

Carefully placed upon the future,
it tips from the breeze and skims away,
frail thing of words, this valentine,
so far to sail. And if you find it
caught in the reeds, its message blurred,
the thought that you are holding it
a moment is enough for me.

—TED KOOSER, *Valentines*

A BOX

of

DARKNESS

PRELUDE

Parsque est meminisse doloris.
"It is part of grief to remember."

—OVID

The Sunday after Easter dawns bitter cold, but at least Cape Cod is sunny and there is no wind. Yesterday my son Nathaniel removed the winter plastic from his nineteen-foot open boat, scrubbed the hull, and polished the fittings. This morning he hitched up the trailer and towed the boat from his house outside Boston to Woods Hole, where the other three children—Sarah, Andrew, and Alexander—and I have assembled on the town dock. We are bundled in down, fleece, and Gor-Tex, knowing it will be even colder on the open water.

Sarah has brought a hundred daffodils and tulips from Connecticut, nestled in a large carton; Natty has a thermos of hot tea. Andrew casts off and the boat slips away, the bow turning toward Vineyard Sound. Martha's Vineyard lies on our left, Naushon Island on our right. We are heading to Tarpaulin Cove off Naushon, five miles down the Sound.

We are just passing the Woods Hole Oceanographic Institution when I look for the square, gray box, deceptively heavy, that holds Upton's ashes. I don't see it in the cockpit, or in the small cabin.

"Where's Upton?" I ask.

Four pairs of blue eyes meet mine.

"On the front hall table at Aunt Joanie's?"

We all start to laugh, a quiet, guilty laugh at first that soon gets raucous. Natty turns the boat around and we head back to the dock. How could we have forgotten Upton? Easy. We forgot him because he wasn't here to remind us. Sarah drives back to the house and we try again.

This time, we make it to Tarpaulin Cove. Natty heads close in to the curve of the northeast shore and cuts the engine. Suddenly the air is still and almost warm. The empty, weathered house, the barn, and the outhouse stand stark vigil on a windswept rise behind the beach. The nearest house is four miles away, and today, in March, ours is the only boat in view. For over thirty years we have been lucky guests on this privately owned island.

Upton always said that being at the Cove was like living in the eighteenth century—no electricity, indoor plumbing, telephone, or cars. Time slowed down, and we paid attention to the smallest details of daily life: washing ourselves and our clothes with water pumped by hand from the well, taking care of trash and garbage, trimming the Aladdin lamps, preparing food using as little gas as possible. Even planning meals took extra care because at the Cove, we used what was there and what was about to spoil, harvested what was in the garden or in the sea. Running to the store meant leaving the island, an all-day event. We lived by the sun, pinching each other to stay awake until nine every night so we wouldn't wake up before five.

Natty's boat drifts lazily across the clear water, held in the crescent of white beach, while memories from past summers lap like the waves on the hull. We haven't planned a ceremony, but one evolves.

"There's Pa's wind vane on the fence post."

"And the screen door he built from scraps."

"Remember when he discovered all the wood at the French Watering Place, and towed it back behind the whaler?"

That was the summer Upton decided to rebuild the deck by the back door, a complicated project in a house with no electricity, on an island without cars or shops.

"Remember when he got the toilet to work again? That project took two years."

"No, three."

The plumbing at the Cove is far from modern, with an outhouse, a sun-shower, and a well. There was indoor plumbing, once; the airy bathroom and generous claw-foot bathtub attest to this. But there was no hot water, and the toilet hadn't worked for years. Because we relied on a small Briggs & Stratton gas engine in the cellar to pump well water into the house once or twice a week, we used water sparingly to save on fuel. Even if the toilet didn't leak, insufficient pressure would have made normal flushing out of the question. But, said Upton, if the leaky pipes to and from the toilet were replaced, we could at least use the john at night and have a single flush in the morning. The older we got, the less we enjoyed going downstairs and across the grass to the outhouse in the middle of the night, especially in the teeth of a nor'easter. Upton steadfastly set to work on the pipes, and three summers later, we celebrated Flush Day. Upton chilled a bottle of champagne in the gas refrigerator and made a hazelnut torte, grinding the nuts by hand in the Mouli. I put on my pearls, and we waltzed up and down the sandy hall on bare feet to Strauss, played on the out-of-tune piano by a visiting concert pianist.

The boat is almost in front of the house now, and I spot the old pier piling on the beach and remember the long-ago night I spent wrapped in a soggy towel, my back against the rotting wood. The house had been full of visitors and children, and after dinner in our bedroom, Upton, mean from too much whiskey, turned on me.

"You're a big phony. A social climber!" He came close and raised his hand.

I'd seen Upton drunk—almost every night he had too much to drink—but this was the first time I was ever afraid of him. I took off for the beach in my nightgown, figuring that without an audience he would stop ranting and soon pass out. I could have crept back later and slipped into bed beside him, but I needed the night alone to sort things out. Upton had crossed a line. Alone on the beach, I realized that I could no longer ignore his anger. An ounce too much of bourbon was all it took for him to erupt. Sarah had just turned thirteen; Alex was seven, and Andrew and Natty were eleven and nine. I would have to figure out a way to keep us all safe.

Now, as the wind and tide take Natty's boat toward the lighthouse bluffs, I also remember sweet afternoons when the children were off fishing or sailing and Upton and I would spread our towels behind the boulders, make salty love and lie together in the sun, the southwest wind caressing our skin. I think of the nights when the lighthouse beam would flash at one-minute intervals on the wall above our bed while we came together as quietly as possible, inevitably betrayed by the rhythmic screech of rusty bedsprings.

Closer to shore now, we see two cows grazing on the tawny grasses up beside the lighthouse. On the beach below, a large coyote appears, sees the boat, and stops to sniff the air. He decides we are nothing to him, and trots off, king of the Cove. Natty looks at his watch, at the buoy beyond the rocks, and finally out at the cold, blue Sound, as if fixing his position with the land and tide.

"Mom, I think we should do it right here."

That's when we spot a colony of harbor seals on the rocks ahead. They watch us and we watch them. Finally, one slithers off his rock and swims up to the boat, gazing at us with round, dark eyes. He waits while I open the box. When I let go of the first handful of ashes, the wind catches them and blows them back at us. Some land, sweet and salty, on my tongue; my last taste of Upton. The next handful lands in the water. Caught by the sun, the ashes begin to sparkle as they slowly drift away from the boat. Then it is the children's turn, everyone tossing Upton into the sea while the seal looks gravely on. We toss the flowers in next. Suddenly, without a ripple, the seal dives, a fleeting shadow beneath the milky cloud. We are done, but still stand, transfixed by the nebula of winking ashes that continues to drift just inches below the surface of the water, surrounded now by a fleet of bobbing tulips and daffodils.

Just before Natty starts the engine he says he has something to sing. "I heard it on the radio driving down this morning, an old Mississippi John Hurt song." He says this with a gleam in his eyes and a touch of shyness in his voice so familiar I hold tight to the side of the boat. I listen to "Let the Mermaids Flirt with Me," a bluesy ballad so appropriate to this little boatful of mourners, and think of the nights when Upton took out his guitar and sang to all of us, with that same tender playfulness— "Sloop John B," "Shenandoah," "Jamaica Farewell." Natty's words settle on the water, the seals watch from the rocks, and slowly the boat turns and noses out into the Sound.

A breeze is picking up and I hunch into my old down jacket. It's all over. The hard years of Upton's drinking and clinical depression, his exhausting and relentless struggle with emotions— his and everyone else's, these are finished. I think of his increasing isolation in life, and of his new, final isolation in death. What do I really know of Upton? What do I know of his life? Of our life together? What do I know that I didn't know I knew until now?

Mary Oliver's "The Uses of Sorrow" runs through my head:

> Someone I loved once gave me
> a box full of darkness.
>
> It took me years to understand
> that this, too, was a gift.

The box that held Upton's ashes sits beside me, empty, swept clean by the wind on the sunny deck of Natty's boat. But I'm still holding that other box in my heart, the one full of darkness.

Upton and Sally.

Cambridge, 1956.

1

*We cannot tell the story of anything without
telling the story of everything.*

—THOMAS BERRY

VERMONT, MARCH 23, 2008

My husband, Upton Birnie Brady, was born on Easter Sunday, April 17, 1938, at the Georgetown University Hospital in Washington, D.C. His mother, Madee (Mah-dee, short for Mother dear), used to speak of this confluence with wonder. Cigarette between her fingers, she would tell how her young husband, Francis, had come to the hospital fresh from Mass, his arms full of violets. Susie, six; Ellen, almost four; and fifteen-month-old Francis, called Buff, were at home with their stuffed bunnies and their grandmother. "To be born on Easter," Madee would say, smoke circling her head, "on the Feast of the Resurrection, is to be twice blessed."

Now it is Easter again and the house in Vermont is bursting with our grown children and their children, everyone painting eggs at the dining room table. The ham is in the oven. The jelly beans have been hidden. There is a foot of snow outside, and not a violet anywhere. The adult children are coping. But I am in a bubble of disbelief, which keeps bursting when I don't see Upton anywhere. The chair where he sits with the *Times* crossword puzzle is empty. On his desk, untouched, lies the manuscript he was editing, his wry comments (two in Latin!) so neatly penciled in the margins. Upton's ordinary, everyday handwriting is as legible and well-proportioned as his Chancery italic on handmade Christmas tags. His final shopping list—*dishwash, steak, pots*—remains intact on the refrigerator door. His slippers are waiting on the floor by his side of the bed.

While I notice these things, the children are urging me to come up with a plan for his memorial service. Our eldest son, Andrew, his wife, Mari, and their two young children have come all the way from San Francisco, and it would save them two thousand dollars if we could do everything within three weeks. Upton always said he wanted to be buried at sea, and we've agreed to scatter his ashes the following weekend. But I truly do not know what Upton would want us to do for a public memorial service, where he would want it to be, or even if he would want one at all. And then the thought crosses my mind that it doesn't really matter what Upton would want; we are doing this for the living, not for him. We just have trouble saying it. We have trouble saying many things.

Three nights ago, Natty was the first to get here. Upton's body was taken away by the undertaker at ten, and Natty arrived at midnight. We had a beer, and I told him how Upton had had a bath late in the day, as he frequently did, but then hadn't come down to watch the weather. Upton never liked watching the news, but he always watched the weather, every night at six-fifteen. I had heard the water sluicing down the pipes around six, and when the weather came on, I wondered why he still hadn't come downstairs.

Afterward, I put the gratin in the oven, set the table, and went up to check on him. The bathroom door was closed, a strip of light coming from the bottom. I knew as I knocked and called out, breathing in the piney scent of rosemary oil from the bath salts, that something was wrong. I didn't wait for a reply, just opened the door, and there he was, clean and sweet and dry, his torso in the empty tub, his legs hanging over the side, his strong feet pink, each toenail smooth and nicely shaped. I tried to picture him perched on the edge of the tub, trying to catch his breath after the long hot soak. His heart must have stopped, not enough oxygen, then a quick collapse and gentle slide back into the tub. His blue eyes were closed, and his face so beautifully serene. No body fluids, no bruises, no life; just an overwhelming peace.

I told Natty how my neighbor Kitty had stayed with me while kind men streamed into the house: paramedics, police, the medical examiner, the undertaker. I told him my answer when the paramedics asked me if they should continue their efforts to bring Upton back to life; I knew that even if they were miraculously successful in getting his heart to work again, no one could restore Upton's brain, oxygen-deprived for at least twenty minutes.

Natty listened while I told him about the day, unexpectedly Upton's and my last together. Unexpectedly, because even though Upton had recently been diagnosed with emphysema, and had a history of heart problems, he was on medication and his short-term prognosis was good.

It had snowed all night and most of the day. Upton, wedded to his daily routine and usually undaunted by slippery roads, decided at ten not to get the mail, and at twelve-thirty, not even to go out for his usual lunch at the Co-op. In the soft daylight of falling snow, we polished off Sunday's asparagus soup, our backs warmed by the woodstove. We talked about the books we were working on and the taxes that were soon due. Upton cooked Mondays through Thursdays. He hated leftovers and shopped every day for that night's supper when he went out for lunch. Since he hadn't gone out, I offered to turn Sunday's baked ham into supper with leeks, potatoes, and a little cheese, and he was grateful.

"I've been cold all day," he said. "If you cook, I can have a nice hot bath before dinner."

We talked about Easter, coming up soon, and where we would go to celebrate the victory of life over death. Our beloved and liberal pastor had retired suddenly a few years ago, driven out by spurious gossip of gay activities, and his humorless replacement made both of us crazy with his ultraconservative doctrine.

"Let's drive down to Cambridge and go to St. Paul's," suggested Upton. "We could stop for lunch on the way back."

A fine plan. St. Paul's had been Upton's church while he was at Harvard and again, five years later, when we moved back to Cambridge from New York. I received my religious instruction at St. Paul's, and six months later, made my First Communion there, a brand-new Catholic, and mother of three small children. St. Paul's was also home to the Boston Boy Choir, and blessed with extraordinary music.

But a few minutes after suggesting we go to St. Paul's, Upton changed his mind. "You know, I don't want to be seen in any Roman Catholic church. Let's just stay here."

Both of us were disgusted by the rash of reports of rampant sexual abuse, and furious at the way the Church continued to protect its pederast priests. But there was also sorrow in Upton's voice, and I knew he missed the liturgy and the liturgical calendar that had been so central throughout his almost seventy years.

Upton would deliberately astonish people he barely knew by saying he had been raised in a Benedictine monastery, as if he'd been a foundling, left in the care of the good brothers. A colorful story, but the truth is that his father was the lay headmaster of the Portsmouth Priory (now Portsmouth Abbey) School in Rhode Island. The Bradys lived in an eighteenth-century farmhouse on the Priory grounds, where the sound of the chapel bell measured their days from lauds to compline. The Church was in the air they breathed, its sacrificial doctrine embedded in their flesh and blood.

A few minutes later, Upton put his soupspoon down. "You know," he said, blue eyes fixed on the snow, "when I come back to this world, I think I'd like to come back as a stone."

"A stone?"

He turned his gaze on me. "Stones are peaceful. Don't you think that would be a good way to return?"

Why was he thinking of returning, when he was still right here, with me? I didn't say that. Nor did I mention that it would be cold to be a stone today, in this snow. I didn't say that maybe stones don't have feelings. I just nodded and said, "Yes, very peaceful."

I talked until Natty and I were both spent. It was time for bed, something I'd been dreading. I looked at my son, standing in the kitchen, solid and robust.

"Natty, what will I do? Where will I sleep?"

He gave me a stern, blue-eyed stare. "Mom, if you ever want to sleep in that bed again, you'd better do it now."

Natty was right. I spent what was left of the night in Upton's and my old spool bed, with his clean scent still on the pillow, and the terrain of his body visible in the hollows of our old mattress.

BOSTON, JUNE 1956

I first met Upton Brady at the Boston Cotillion. In May, I graduated from Foxhollow, a small boarding school for girls in Lenox,
Massachusetts, and a week later, I turned seventeen. In September, I would start my freshman year at Barnard College in New
York. But on that June night in the ornate ballroom of the old
Copley Plaza with its gilded chairs and potted palms, I was a wary
Boston debutante in a rustling, long white dress and creamy kid
gloves that stopped at my shoulders. There were a hundred of us,
each with shiny hair, our teeth straight, lined up to proceed on our
father's arm down the length of the ballroom to the six matrons
waiting to welcome us into Boston society. Two of these women
with their glittering diamond rings and pearl chokers were mothers of friends from school. They'd given me rides in their station
wagons; I'd seen them in blue jeans, raking leaves and scouring
their kitchens. And now, as the master of ceremonies announced
my name, I curtsied to them—not just a little bob of a curtsy, but
all the way to the floor. It was hard not to giggle.

George, my Cotillion escort, home for the summer from Yale,
was a good friend, not a boyfriend. Like me, he was tongue-in-
cheek about the debutante ritual. What's more, he was a quick,
sure-footed partner, making me feel like Cyd Charisse as we circled and dipped beneath the winking chandeliers. Unlike most
couples that night, we were there to dance, not flirt; I think that's
why Upton cut in, for the dancing.

"Upton Brady." He bowed slightly as he took my gloved
hand, and I thought he clicked his heels, though it happened so
fast I wasn't sure.

"Sally Ryder," I said, caught suddenly by the bluest eyes I'd ever seen.

Most men at dancing parties were much too tall for me, their feet too big. But not this blond, fine-boned Harvard sophomore with startlingly blue eyes. When he put his hand firmly against my back and propelled me across the polished floor, our bodies fit, leg to leg, pelvis to pelvis. I instinctively knew what his next step would be. When, without any warning, he let me drop almost to the floor in a dip, I didn't miss a beat. And when someone cut in a few minutes later, I was both sorry and glad—sorry the dance with Upton was over, but glad it was clear I was no wallflower. Maybe, I thought, he will cut in again.

And he did, several times that night, each time asking me to tell him my name, one more time. Upton Brady, impeccably turned out in his grandfather's tails, boiled shirt with gold studs and wing collar, was charming, even when tipsy; even when he couldn't remember my name. It seemed as if he could physically telegraph to my body whatever steps he was inventing on the dance floor, making each swooping waltz and sultry tango feel as natural as breathing.

At the many coming-out parties that followed the Cotillion, Upton would often appear—a self-proclaimed "deb's delight." He would cut in, and skim me across the floor, tails whipping around his narrow hips. At every party, when the music stopped, he would give me a slightly sheepish look, his eyes too bright. "I'm terribly sorry," he'd say, his hand still firm against the small of my back, "but I've forgotten your name again."

My debutante year sped by, with many dancing parties and many dancing partners—handsome, eligible young men who, unlike Upton, did remember my name. But Upton was the one I looked for.

The summer of 1956, right after the Cotillion, I was an apprentice at the Cambridge Drama Festival, a summer theater company that put on three high-powered Equity shows: *Saint Joan,* starring Siobhán McKenna; *The Beggar's Opera,* with Shirley Jones and Jack Cassidy; and *Henry the Fifth,* with Michael Wager, Douglass Watson, and Felicia Monteleagre, who was married to Leonard Bernstein. Overnight, I became more Bohemian than debutante, my silky pageboy now replaced by saucy gamin fringe.

Two of the producers, Bryant Haliday and William Morris Hunt, were founders of the Brattle Theatre Company, an avant-garde, professional company in Cambridge. Haliday and several of the actors were openly homosexual, something no one paid much attention to. I had never known anyone who was queer—at least, not that I knew of. I didn't even know what it was they did, just that it was forbidden. Bryant had a beautiful young French boy, ten or eleven, living with him. I didn't know what their relationship was, but there were hints of sex that made me uneasy, and made me think there was something sinister about Bryant. I never felt comfortable around him, but the other homosexual men were more familiar to me, easy to be around, and I soon stopped thinking of them as different from any of the other assorted theater people.

I met Nikos at the end of that summer at a typical Cambridge party in a hot, crowded, third-floor garret. I was sitting on top of the refrigerator wearing a red Lanz dress sprinkled with valentines. Nikos appeared, so tall his dark eyes were nearly level with mine from my perch. He looked like a young Gregory

Peck, only darker and even more handsome, his lips curved in a classic archaic smile. Nikos, with his laundered English shirts and formal, European manners, was not a bit like the other scruffy, sandaled, Harvard Square actor/playwrights, and I wanted him to ask me out. But Harvard Summer School was ending, and Nikos was on his way to Europe before classes started up again in the fall.

In September, I began my freshman year at Barnard. Nikos and I didn't meet again until the following year, when I was back in Cambridge. I spent far more time at Yale and Princeton my freshman year than in classrooms or the library, and in June, the Barnard deans wisely suggested that I take a year or two off. I moved back in with my parents, learned to type, and got a job at Harvard with time off to study acting at Boston University. Joan Baez was in my acting class. She, too, lived with her parents, in nearby Belmont, and three mornings a week she'd pick me up on her Vespa and off we'd go. For the next two years, I acted in the Poets' Theatre and in various Harvard productions, where Nikos and I rediscovered each other and began to go out, casually at first, and soon with a new fire. Nikos paid attention to me, to my clothes, to my stories about growing up in Woods Hole, to my theatrical ambitions. He seemed hungry to know everything about me, and made me feel as if I had a wealth of treasure to offer him, bright gems to delight another person, something I'd never felt before.

His senior year, Nikos moved off campus into an apartment with two classmates, a grown-up arrangement with separate bedrooms and no parietal hours, unlike in the Harvard dorms. One of his roommates had a live-in girlfriend whose diaphragm sat carelessly on the shelf above the bathroom sink. I was still a virgin, a "nice girl" who couldn't imagine chatting with my doctor—also my mother's doctor—about birth control. I would eye the diaphragm, thinking there was something slutty about such open premarital sex. Weren't we supposed to "save ourselves" for our husbands? My relationship with Nikos intensified; I stopped seeing other men, awash in the delirium of first love and dissolving boundaries, in believing I "belonged" to someone else.

Nikos brought me to Rye, New York, to visit his elegant Greek parents. Their house, on the edge of a famous country club, couldn't have been more different from my parents' house in Cambridge, with its motley collection of well-thumbed books, scarred family furniture, balding Oriental rugs, and even a few dark portraits of ancestors. At the house in Rye, luminous French Impressionist paintings with their own recessed ceiling lights glowed on the walls, and my feet sank into snow-white carpets. I enjoyed Nikos's parents, but not his unease when he was with them. In Rye, even his posture was different. He hunched over, no longer six feet two; he was never without a cigarette, and worst of all, he had trouble with words; sometimes the effort of speaking seemed almost unbearable. Alone with me, or with his friends, Nikos was a gifted talker with curious stories and the wit of a wordsmith. But when he was in his father's house, he was nearly mute. Luckily he would soon make his own, separate life.

His parents took me skiing in Vermont and to family parties, one on an enormous, sleek, well-staffed yacht in Long Island Sound, and others at lavish Westchester houses where soignée women glittered around gaming tables, and prosperous Greek shipping magnates placed bets far larger than my Harvard salary on the green baize. I went with them several times to the Greek

Orthodox church in Stamford, where I hoped that in time, the pageantry of ritual and language could bring me closer to this exotic clan, instead of making a wider separation. I could easily imagine giving up the familiar words of the Book of Common Prayer and the King James Bible for Greek chants intoned in their ancient modes. I daydreamed of a future with Nikos, a cosmopolitan life with writers, actors, dancers in New York or London; of holidays with our beautiful dark-haired little children on the Greek island of Siros, where his aunties still lived. My serviceable French would become fluent, and I would study modern Greek. It wouldn't be long before I'd be completely assimilated into this international community, Yankee roots and all.

His parents invited me to sit with them at Harvard commencement in June 1959, where, to my surprise, the Latin Orator was none other than Upton Brady. He cut as neat a figure before a thousand people in his academic robe as he had in evening clothes, dancing in an intimate Beacon Hill ballroom three years earlier. But this time, my partner was Nikos, not Upton, and I was shocked to feel a flicker of regret. I watched Upton stride across the platform, blond hair shining in the morning sun, declaiming in fluent Latin, and wondered if the past three years might have been very different for me had he only remembered my name.

That fall I went back to Barnard as a day student, living with my sister, Joan, and her husband, Peter, and their new baby on East Seventy-sixth Street. Nikos was also in New York, at work on a novel in a small apartment on East Eighty-ninth. After he graduated, his father had pressured him to go into the shipping business, but Nikos refused, wanting only to write. Finally, his father agreed to subsidize him for a year.

What initially sounded like a generous gesture came with tremendous expectations, and not surprisingly, Nikos's writing turned sluggish and forced. He would retreat into what he called a "blue funk," where he was inaccessible to me, brooding and dark, but never unkind. I knew I was not the cause of his suffering, and at best could only temporarily relieve it. Yet I was absolutely certain that when we married, when we began to spend the rest of our lives together, the blinding light of our love would sear his darkness, reduce it to ashes. We were not yet lovers, not completely. I still didn't have a diaphragm, and the idea of condoms was repellent—the only ones I'd ever seen were used, discarded in parking lots like toilet paper. I wanted sex to be pure, unsullied, and so our lovemaking was always cut short by the looming fear of my getting pregnant.

When the year was over and his book was still unwritten, Nikos decided to go to Harvard Graduate School and get his master's degree in teaching. He moved back to Cambridge, and I left college for good, determined to pursue an acting career. I moved out of Joan and Peter's apartment and into a sunny fourth-floor walk-up a few blocks away that I shared with my boarding school friend Libby. By day I helped philanthropic socialites run gala benefits to support the Henry Street Settlement, squeezing in dance classes and Broadway auditions whenever I could. By night—not every night but often—it was dinner at "21," the Italian Pavilion, Le Veau d'Or, or noisy P.J. Clarke's, depending on who had invited me. A glamorous life for a single twenty-one-year-old. It was 1960, and I dated many, slept with none, and dreamed of married life with my true love, Nikos Lambrinides, and the next time he would come down from Cambridge.

In January, I came up from New York to Cambridge to see Nikos. His apartment near his old Harvard dorm was filled with pictures of me, like a gallery. We were geographically more apart than we'd ever been, and yet we were closer in every other way. The weekend was short, with my time split between Nikos and my parents. At night, I slept at home, in my childhood bed, after spending several hours with Nikos, on his. I returned to New York late Sunday and had barely gotten into the apartment when the phone rang. It was Nikos.

"Will you marry me?"

I said yes.

For that one glorious night, we were engaged. I called home to share my happy news. My father answered. Nikos had spoken with him already, and Daddy gave me his blessing. Then he handed the phone to my mother. I expected that she, too, would be pleased, but my mother clearly was not.

Raised poor on the wrong side of the tracks in the backwater town of Middleboro, Massachusetts, Mummy never tried to hide her aspirations for my sister and me. She was thrilled when Joan married Peter, a well-born, well-heeled New Yorker, and I knew she'd always hoped I would choose a Boston Brahmin, someone like Thomas Jefferson Coolidge, whom I briefly dated. Nevertheless, Mummy had always seemed very taken with respectful, polite Nikos. She'd even put on a graduation lunch for his family. Yet now, when the chips were down, she clearly disapproved. Finally, in a mean, clipped voice, she said she guessed she could learn to love a "little black baby." Those were her words. She must have been referring to the color of Nikos's hair, since his skin is lighter than my own. But it didn't matter. What she meant was Nikos was Greek. Well, she would have to work that out.

After talking to me and to my father, Nikos jumped into the Alfa Romeo and sped to Rye, to give his parents the news before they left for Florida. I would see him the next day, after I got home from work. That night, I lay in bed in a kind of ecstatic stupor. My path was suddenly so clear and so right; not even a hairline crack of doubt. We would spend the rest of our lives together, Nikos and I, Greek shipping heir and Boston debutante. Our different backgrounds would be our dowries, our gifts to each other. On Monday soon after I got home from work, Nikos came to the apartment. He did not bound up the stairs like a jubilant bridegroom, he came slowly and quietly, his shoulders stooped. When he took me in his arms, he held me far enough away so he could look into my eyes. His own looked very black, with a hint of fury; his beautiful soft lips were set in a hard line. I had never seen him like this before.

"I talked to my parents," he said, each word falling separately, hard as rocks.

"And?"

"They said no. Absolutely not."

"But they like me. They love me!"

Nikos shook his head. "You are not Greek."

"So what?"

"They will disinherit me. They say I am not ready, that I am unstable. And you are not Greek. I cannot do it now. I can't marry you."

How could they have been so kind to me, so welcoming? How could they have pretended they were fond of me? I had even believed that Mr. and Mrs. Lambrinides thought fortune smiled when Nikos and I fell in love. I was twenty years old, naïve, and betrayed, first by my own mother and then by both his parents, which in a way was even worse. All because he was Greek and I wasn't.

Nikos and I had gone as far as we could without some sort of commitment and now we were stuck. My father suggested we call a six-month moratorium, during which we would have no direct contact with one another. Then, in June, we could see each other again. We reluctantly agreed to no visits, no phone calls, no letters—just occasional indirect communication through my parents or Libby, my roommate. I didn't eat, couldn't sleep, and began a winter of recurring staph infections, all of which I attributed to a broken heart.

This is the state I was in when Upton waltzed back into my life.

Libby, the eldest of eight in a socially prominent Catholic family, knew the elusive Upton not only from her years at Radcliffe but also from Portsmouth Priory, where several of her brothers had been students. She knew Upton's two brothers as well. When she spoke of Upton, it was in the tender, tentative way of possible lovers. But aside from one or two postcards from the Caribbean, where he was winding up his two-year Navy ROTC duty, there didn't seem to be much going on between them.

One January day, Lib came home from her job at Sotheby's with the handsomest man I'd ever seen: Upton's brother Buff, also blond and blue-eyed but sixteen months older than Upton. Buff had recently been in the Navy, too, but he had not finished college and was living frugally at the YMCA while he looked for a job.

"You can't live at the Y," announced Lib. "There's no kitchen!"

Buff was soon hired by Air France to work nights in air traffic control, and he moved in with us. It was a perfect arrangement.

He would come home from work around seven, when we were just waking up. He'd make coffee for Lib and me and a martini for himself; we'd go off to work and he'd climb into one of our unmade beds. When we came home around six, the beds were made, dinner was in the oven, and a glass of wine waited for each of us. On Saturdays, he and Lib went off to Confession at St. Jean Baptiste, the Roman Catholic church on Seventy-sixth Street, and came back with a kind of lightness that I both envied and didn't understand. On Sundays, they skipped breakfast and, missals in their hands, went to Mass, Lib with a black lace mantilla stuffed in her pocket. Hatless and fueled by coffee and toast, I'd go alone to the Episcopal church around the corner.

I had been bereft of Nikos for a few weeks when Upton called from Norfolk, where his ship had docked, asking Lib if he could come for the weekend. First, I was excited by the thought of seeing Upton again after so many years. Then I thought of Nikos, my true love, the one I was waiting for. And finally I admitted that Upton was coming for Lib, as her boyfriend. Or so I assumed from the way Lib brightened when she answered the phone.

With that call, the dynamics in our apartment changed. We were suddenly four almost every other weekend, very chaste, the boys in the living room, trading off between the sofa and a sleeping bag on the floor, the girls in the bedroom. The climate was rife with sexual energy, but I was more focused on Nikos's absence than on Upton's presence. Sometimes while we were drinking and dancing or playing backgammon the phone would ring, person-to-person to Lib from Nikos. It was odd to hear her talking to him in the bedroom, while I laughed in the living room with Upton and Buff.

We mostly stayed home on the weekends. There was plenty of rum, bourbon, and wine; there was backgammon and poker; there was music. And dancing, always dancing. Upton, fresh from the Caribbean, came with LPs of steel bands and stories of dancing at The Gate in Saint Thomas and beach days at Magens Bay. His face changed when the music started, blue eyes suddenly veiled and distant as if he were somewhere else, with palm trees and gentle breezes. Even his lips were different, not quite pursed but gently full, small, rhythmic breaths escaping between them. The merengue pulsed through his lower body, his pelvis and legs becoming almost fluid. When he held me, his hand firm on the small of my back, our bodies very close, our feet quick and light, I felt we could dance like this on the rim of a canyon or the bowsprit of a boat in heavy seas. We wouldn't fall, but we would taste the danger. I couldn't get enough of this new drug.

Buff, taller than Upton and an extraordinary athlete (he'd been seeded at Forest Hills), was not a natural dancer. Odd, because he was much more physical than Upton, generous with hugs or a gentle massage on your neck. Something, maybe the closeness of our bodies and the insistence of the music, or maybe simply Upton's natural grace, made Buff reluctant and more of a dancing clown, gently mocking Upton's showmanship. Lib and I danced with one Brady, flirted with another. Buff seemed to favor Lib, Lib seemed to favor Upton, Upton was supposed to favor Lib—after all, he was her guest—but after a month or so I began to wonder if maybe it was me he danced for. I think I was a little in love with all three of them.

Every Sunday, hangovers notwithstanding, they traipsed off to Mass, and soon I went with them, learning when to stand and sit and kneel and genuflect. The liturgy was still in Latin then, but the translation of the Canon was not very different from the Book of Common Prayer that I'd grown up with. No matter, I was not allowed to receive the Eucharist, and stood alone in the aisle to let them pass, heads bowed, on their way to the altar.

"Unless you join the Church, you won't be saved." Buff repeated this to me more than once. And when I asked what "saved" really meant, both he and Upton had the same dire answer.

"You will never be in the presence of God."

"Without the Church, you will be doomed to an eternity without God."

They didn't speak of Heaven or Hell; just the presence or absence of God. This wasn't what I'd learned in my Protestant Sunday School, where Hell was a place of eternal torment for evildoers like Hitler and Jack the Ripper, and Heaven the kingdom where everyone we knew ended up. It had never crossed my mind that salvation was for Catholics only, that they were the chosen ones. This seemed to be the heart of the matter for Upton and Buff, and even Lib, and it remains for me, fifty years later, an insurmountable difference in belief. But back then, drawn to the mystery of the sacraments, to the banks of red and blue candles, incense, Gregorian chant, rosaries, even to the scraps of black lace on bowed heads, I yearned to join the club. I followed Buff, Lib, and Upton to Mass every Sunday, a reluctant outsider who nonetheless fasted first (nothing to eat or drink from midnight on, except water) and dove into celebratory breakfasts afterward. Holy days of obligation and first Fridays: these, too, were woven into our lives.

I had barely heard of Evelyn Waugh or *Brideshead Revisited*, but all three of them knew the book almost as well as they knew their Gospels. Evelyn Waugh had even visited the Priory, gone to Mass with his large ear trumpet, and had tea poured by Madee at the Manor House. Upton, Buff, and Lib talked about Sebastian Flyte and Lady Marchmain the way they talked about the monks, gossip steeped in the heady power of the Church.

As soon as I started to read, I could see the connections. The Flytes were English nobility, and rich. The Bradys, though poor, were "raised rich," as Upton liked to remind people. They went to fancy schools, wore fancy hand-me-downs, cavorted with fancy people. Madee was the daughter of West Point graduate General Upton Birnie, former Captain of Field Artillery. She had grown up in China and the Philippines, with amahs and finger bowls. The General had worn the very same tailcoat Upton had worn when we first met, only the General had worn it to the White House. Brideshead may have been a castle with its own family chapel, but the chapel next to the Brady farmhouse came with its own priory of monks.

The Flytes were charming, erudite, well-mannered—at least most of the time—as were the Bradys. Everybody drank too much. The Flytes had a rigid structure of right and wrong, black and white, enforced by the Church. I thought about this, and began to see Upton and Buff in a new light. Unlike my view of the world, which was not black and white but gray with possibilities, choices, and unknown promise, the Brady boys saw things as absolute. There was one way, and one way only. The Bradys, like the Flytes, were special, favored, apart from the rest of the world. This came with burdens, with standards to live up to. Failure was not an option. I wondered how they all managed this pressure.

In *Brideshead,* even the smallest act became a ritual. In the fourth-floor walk-up on Second Avenue, Upton would swirl his martini and hold it up to the light, attentive as a priest consecrating the wine. Every Saturday morning, the boys would insist we all clean the apartment, just the way every Saturday growing up they had all cleaned the Priory farmhouse. They bought several albums of Gilbert and Sullivan to brightly urge us on, another part of the Brady cleaning ritual. They polished their shoes before Mass, and always had freshly ironed (by them) handkerchiefs peeking out of the breast pockets of their blue blazers. (Lib and I didn't even have an ironing board in the apartment until Buff bought one.) Everywhere I looked, I spotted a ritual; it was all so unlike my own informal family of just my sister and me and two fairly ordinary parents.

Guilt governed the Flytes and the Bradys, guilt that they had sinned against Christ. The guilt in the house I grew up in was from sinning against people, mainly from disobeying or even disagreeing with my mother. It had nothing to do with God. I would apologize, possibly be punished, and wait for the guilt to fade. With the Catholic Bradys, the burden of sin was huge. Sin could rob you of everything good, of the presence of God. Sin demanded immediate expiation through the act of confession, followed by the gift of absolution. Total forgiveness, every Saturday, as long as you truly intended not to repeat the sin. I wanted to be inside this elite, sacred circle, where everyone played by the same well-known rules: a safe world made up of absolutes, of right and wrong, a world where you could be saved over and over again by ceremonial sacraments. I might even be able to stop questioning the truth of only one path to eternal salvation.

Sebastian Flyte was harder to explain. In spite of the

Church—or because of it?—Sebastian was a drunk. And probably a homosexual. Certainly Waugh hints at this, and Waugh himself was "queer," a "fairy," terms we used in 1961. When I tried to talk to the sunny Brady boys about Sebastian Flyte, they looked uncomfortable and shrugged, rum punches and Pall Malls in their hands.

"Cigarette?"

"Can I freshen your drink?"

I wondered if Buff might be homosexual. Once in a while, there was something about his laugh, and a veiled sadness in his blue eyes. But there was nothing effeminate in his strong athlete's body, or in the way he moved, the only outward signs I knew to look for. Just a quiet remove that hinted of secrets, which drew me to him. He had none of Upton's dazzling repartee; he didn't sweep people into his orbit the way Upton did. Sometimes he seemed almost apologetic, but I never knew for what.

June finally came to an end, and soon afterward, our household on Second Avenue would dissolve. Lib was sailing off on the *Queen Mary* to work at Sotheby's in London, Buff landed a job working with computers at MIT, and Upton was newly mustered out of the Navy. I wanted to keep the apartment but would have to find a new roommate. Most important, the imposed separation between Nikos and me would be coming to an end.

Nikos: I couldn't wait to see him, but I was also uneasy. The six-month retreat I had imagined as a time to meditate on our future seemed now to have been a time more of revelry, with Upton dancing in its center. But surely when Nikos and I were back together, my pulse would stop quickening when I thought of Upton. Wouldn't it? Though a week shy of our six months, we had set aside this weekend because Nikos was leaving right afterward for Greece and we wanted to end the separation before he flew off for the summer. But it would also be the last time Lib, Buff, Upton, and I were all together. Friends had invited the four of us to a house party on Long Island, and I was determined to go.

"Could you pick me up in Oyster Bay on Saturday afternoon?"

"I thought we had a date for Friday."

The surprised disappointment in his voice made me feel I was betraying him. "It's my last night with Lib," I said, not mentioning Upton or Buff.

Friday night and Saturday on Long Island were bittersweet, the end of a brief season when anything had seemed possible, and nothing demanded commitment. I have never been stoic with endings and departures, and this was no exception. Even my wardrobe wasn't quite right. I'd come out by train in shorts, bringing only a bikini and clean underwear. I don't think I really wanted to get all dolled up for Nikos right away; I wanted just to be myself for the first few hours, bare-legged, brown from the sun, no makeup, hair in a ponytail. Back in the city, I would slither into my new silky lemon shift, put on gold beads and earrings, sweep my hair into a French twist, apply a touch of mascara, a dab of Chanel No. 5. But on Saturday afternoon, Nikos would see me unadorned, the way I'd been with Buff and Lib and Upton.

From the shaded terrace overlooking the water, I heard Nikos's little Alfa Romeo Spider crunch up the gravel drive. A quick embrace for Lib and Buff, a wave to Upton, and then I ran across the sun-splashed lawn and into Nikos's arms. I hadn't forgotten his familiar warm kiss, or the comfortable way he folded me against his chest as if I were a child. There was the good smell of his smooth, crisp shirt and the skin beneath it. Nikos brought me back to him so easily, so fast. On the Long Island Expressway, noisy with wind and traffic, I stared at his graceful hands, large and long-fingered on the steering wheel, and resisted the urge to cover them with kisses. I studied his profile, like something on an ancient coin and yet so familiar. I marveled at the way his dark hair curled on the back of his vulnerable, pale neck. I had loved him for three years, which seemed an eternity. He looked back at me, our eyes briefly meeting, and I knew he was still in love with me. Would we pick up where we left off, ready to become engaged, and then to marry? Had his parents changed their minds about me? Wasn't this what I had longed for?

Later, at Orsini's, the glittery, chattering crowd and the red velvet walls made me feel private, as if Nikos and I were in our own bubble. And it was easier to talk with food and drinks to toy with.

"How has it been for you," I asked, "these past six months?"

He drew on his cigarette, took a sip of Dewar's Black and White. "D-d-difficult." Another inhale, exhale. Another sip. "Very d-d-difficult."

I waited; there was clearly more, but Nikos didn't say anything else, just solemnly ground out his cigarette. Finally, he raised his eyes, gave me a guarded look.

"And you?" he asked.

Now it was my turn to look at my plate, light a Marlboro. "I was sick," I said. "Staph. I had my tonsils out."

"I know," he said gently. "Your father told me. And Lib."

"I missed you," I said. It was true, I had missed him, but my words sounded hollow.

"Yes?"

I nodded.

"Were you lonely?"

Ah. That was the hard one to answer. He waited, dark eyes never blinking, while I tried not to think about the rum punches, the dancing, the Mass on Sunday mornings.

Again I nodded, a small nod this time, and reached for his hand. He let me hold it for a second or two, and then slipped it back across the tablecloth to his lap. Respectful, even shy, we were definitely not where we'd left off in December.

"When I talked to Libby," he said quietly, "I heard music and laughter in the background. I wanted to be there."

"Yes. I wanted you there."

Nikos didn't say anything; he looked into my eyes and let my words hang. They had sounded false. Nikos was restrained; he had a new gravity, or maybe just less levity, as if he were suddenly wary of me. And he should have been. For in those six months, without my acknowledging it until now, I had changed. Upton had sucked me into his shimmering aura with words and waltzes, and now, like a junkie, I wanted more. Upton made the air crackle. We had never kissed, but I had felt my body melt against his over and over while the steel band pulsed, and now nothing was the same. I felt myself pulling away from Nikos, and at the same time I wanted him to wrap me in his arms and take me away—from what? I think I wanted Nikos to take me away from Upton.

I didn't know what the next step was, or even, more immediately, what would happen in an hour or two when he brought me back to the apartment, conveniently empty with Lib and the boys still on Long Island. We were very kind with each other that night. He held me, kissed me, smoothed my hair, and I wanted to weep because our old, headlong passion wasn't there. I wanted to weep because I knew it had been replaced by doubt. Nikos left early. We did not end our romance. We had all summer to reflect; maybe when he came back from Greece we would see more clearly where we were, and where we might go.

Twenty-four hours later, Buff and Lib were gone, too. That evening, Upton and I walked along the promenade above the East River, first holding hands (trying to be casual about it, though it felt to me like holding a lightning rod), then settling on a remote bench overlooking the black river. Neither one of us talked. We just looked at the surging water and then at each other until finally, Upton kissed me.

Six months of desire erupted in a single kiss. It was a starting gun going off, the beginning of a marathon, and there was no turning back. Of course I felt guilty and torn, with Nikos still such a huge part of my twenty-one-year-old self. Upton was an intruder, but an intruder I couldn't dismiss. I wanted him to take me, there on the bench above the river. I wanted to make love with him, "go all the way," as we said back then. We walked back to the apartment, his arm around me, hips touching, step by step, every block a sweet agony, until finally, we mounted the three flights of stairs.

Upton, as frenzied as I, was nimble with buttons and zippers, until just at the last minute, when with a moan, he left my bed and climbed into Lib's, only a night table's width away.

"I can't do this," he said. "It's called fornicating. A sin."

Brideshead again. I couldn't believe it. How could I fight this power?

We spent the night in our twin beds, holding hands across the gap. At dawn, I couldn't stand it any longer and slid in beside him, matching my breathing to his, in and out. The rhythm of his chest intensified as his arms tightened around me, then suddenly Upton pushed me away, jumped out of bed and into the shower. Alone on the tangled sheets, I went over what had happened, or what had not happened. Surely Upton had had sex before. Anyone that handsome and that sexy after four years at Harvard and two in the Navy must have had many lovers. But when I asked him over coffee, he told me, shamefaced and embarrassed, that he hadn't.

"Once, in the Navy, there was a prostitute. But nothing happened. I was too drunk." His eyes were on his cigarette while he told me this, his voice very quiet.

Even in 1961, I was shocked. No, Nikos and I had not gone all the way, but we had certainly come close, and I knew Nikos had had considerable experience with women. But Upton, now reading *The New York Times* across from me and smelling of soap, was as virginal as I.

That night, flush with his mustering-out pay, Upton took me to El Morocco. Half hidden by potted palms, we flirted over stingers in the shadowy zebra banquette, making our way between drinks to the mostly deserted dance floor. There, in the dim, circling lights, the band played tangos, merengues, and waltzes as if only for us, my hips as loose as his, each of our legs pressed along the length of the other's as we traveled across the smooth floor. Many stingers and many dances later, we went home to fall into bed—the same bed—exhausted, and chaste.

The next night, we went to the Rendezvous Room in the bowels of the Plaza, not as glamorous as El Morocco but cheaper and cozy, each little round table with its peachy lamp and fringed shade. Again, lots of dancing, lots of stingers, and later, lots of insistent, unconsummated sex. I had become the seducer, Upton the reluctant virgin, aided by alcoholic impotence. Upton called it a "state of suspended animation," which it surely was. And I hoped it wouldn't last much longer. How could it? But I underestimated the power of the Church.

Upton and Sally.
New York, 1961.

2

*We lie on our beds through the ecstatic night, wide
awake, cracked open. There will be no going back.*

—MAY SARTON

Even though this will be our first Easter without church, I know
we have to mark Upton's life and death formally, in a sacred
place. Portsmouth Abbey, on the open, rolling land where both
his parents are buried, overlooking Narragansett Bay, in which
he'd learned to swim and sail; this seems the single, right place. I
call his brother Jeremiah, of all the Bradys the one who has remained in closest touch with the Abbey. Jem has weathered
several serious health problems over the past few years, but he
immediately offers to call the Abbey to see if we can have the
service there on April 5. And he has good ideas about the service itself. I relax a little, now that I have him to help me.

On Easter Monday, Sarah offers to go through Upton's desk,
assess the finances, see where we are with taxes, balance his checkbook. I see Sarah twenty-seven years ago, a freshman at Connecticut College, sitting next to Upton at the kitchen table in

tears as he shows her how to set up a budget. A realistic budget, not one that just looks good.

"Beer," says Upton. "Pizza. You have to put those in."

"I do?" Sarah is shocked.

Upton nods, writing "Beer" on the ledger page in his careful script. "How much do you spend?"

Silence.

"It's nothing to be ashamed of, Sarah. Not something to hide. How much?"

Sarah looks embarrassed. "Um, maybe twenty dollars a month."

"Twenty?" asks Upton. "Or thirty?"

"Um, thirty, I guess."

"Sarah, if you really spend thirty dollars a month on beer, don't put down twenty dollars. Because there won't be any money left for tampons or pizza. You can't have an emotional attachment to money. It's just money."

Sarah learned well from her father. I wish he could see her now, poring over his accounts with her unclouded vision.

From the day we married, Upton insisted on our having separate checking accounts, and on paying all the bills himself. Each month he gave me a check to cover food and household expenses. Whatever incidental money I needed for clothes, bus fare, lipstick, I either earned from various pickup jobs (the first few years we were married, I worked as a very part-time social secretary for two busy New York women) or squeezed from the food allowance. At the time, it seemed right to me that the man, the "head of the household," would handle the money, and I assumed that despite the separate bank accounts, his money was our money.

We had four babies in five and a half years and moved from

New York to Boston. I stayed home with the children—no more part-time work or incidental money. And what Upton gave me for food was no longer enough. When I told him I needed more, when I mentioned our money, he became furious.

"Our money? It is *my* money. And don't you ever forget it." This was the first time I saw Upton icy and tight-lipped. "*My* money." His words rang with emotional attachment. The subject was closed, no more discussion, and I knew I was too scared to open it up again. I would have to find another way to solve my problem.

There wasn't any day care in 1969, and less than a week after I learned that there was only Upton's money, I acquired two new babies to take care of for two grateful working mothers. They gave me their children Monday through Friday, and every Friday afternoon I had two checks, each made out to me. *My money.*

To the end, Upton's money remained a private matter. Sarah has been at his desk all morning, steadily tapping away on his calculator. Finally, she calls me, and it's clear from her voice that there is trouble.

"What's wrong?" I ask, my hand on her slumped shoulders.

"Did you know Pa was over seventy thousand dollars in debt?" She looks up. "Mom?"

Seventy thousand dollars?

"Mom? Did you hear what I just said?"

I can't really grasp what she is saying. *Seventy thousand dollars.*

"They are about to turn off the electricity and the phone!"

I wonder how this can be, because I had given Upton a check every month for my share of these bills. Where had my money gone?

Sarah starts calling all the creditors to tell them Upton has died. She cancels the credit cards. Gradually, as I listen to her make call after call, the extent of the debt begins to sink in, and I have flashes of fear that make me forget, for a second or two, that Upton has died.

I don't know what I will do. The first year we were married, right after Sarah was born, Upton had taken out a term life insurance policy for $100,000, which seemed like a fortune then. But over forty-six years, the principal had dwindled to $25,000, and the value of the dollar had dwindled right along with it. Not only that, Upton had borrowed against it. Yesterday, I gave the undertaker a check for $1,700 just for taking Upton's body from the house to the crematorium. Now I write out three more checks, big ones, for several months of power, heating oil, and telephone service. I feel as though I am teetering on the edge of a black hole. We do not own our house; we have no savings; there is still outstanding debt on both Toyotas. And I am self-employed.

I call the probate court and make a date to bring Upton's will and death certificate to them. My best friend Barbara's husband, a retired lawyer, offers to advise me if I need help, but at the moment, I don't know enough to know what to ask him.

Here is what I do know:

I know we will scatter Upton's ashes this coming weekend. I know there will be a splendid memorial service for Upton at the Portsmouth Abbey in two weeks. There will be beautiful music; Alex and Sarah will speak; Natty and Andrew will read. There will even be lunch afterward in the Abbey refectory, all arranged by Jem and the monks. Not only that, Jem says the cost of the luncheon is covered. Step-by-step, day by day, this is all I can do. And this is enough.

NEW YORK, JULY 1961

Less than a week after Buff moved to Cambridge and Lib set sail for England, Buff telephoned us, announcing that he had proposed to Lib via the High Seas Operator on the old *Queen Mary*. Two days out of New York, with an ocean widening between them, Lib had accepted. Buff and Lib, engaged to be married? Upton and I were stunned. They had no specific date or plans beyond the engagement. Lib didn't quit her London job, nor did Buff quit his job in Cambridge. I thought of the last month we were all together—what had I missed to be so unprepared for this? I couldn't recall even a hint of passion between them. Certainly nothing like the heat that now consumed Upton and me.

Upton went home for a few weeks to see his mother and talk to the Harvard placement office about finding a job. Madee had hoped Upton would go into the foreign service, but he'd failed the orals, and the Harvard career counselor hadn't had much experience placing cum laude classics majors.

"Latin and Greek? Hmm. Maybe something in publishing?"

This turned out to be the right direction, and Upton was soon back in Manhattan, hired as a college traveler by Alfred A. Knopf. He used to call it "peddling textbooks" to sociology and economics professors at colleges in New York, Connecticut, and New Jersey. He drove a "solid-gold Pontiac" (courtesy of Knopf) and moved into a semifurnished studio apartment on East Ninety-second Street, just up from the old Ruppert brewery, a neighborhood redolent of yeasty hops.

A friend of Lib's, Pat, took over Lib's half of the lease and moved in with me in July. The following weekend, Upton and I discovered Fire Island. We left the car in Patchogue and took the ferry to Davis Park, a small community of families with children. There were public toilets and showers, a general store, and the Casino, a restaurant with a jukebox and a listing porch that overlooked the beach. After dinner, and dancing on the porch, we found a deserted stretch of beach and spread out our towels. In seconds, we were covered with mosquitoes so voracious they even bit through our clothes. The only way to escape them was to bury ourselves. We scooped out two shallow graves and covered our bodies with sand and our heads with towels. Level with the sand except for our heads, we were at great risk of being run over by the Jeeps that patrolled the beach all night. But we were also hard to detect, which meant that we didn't get picked up. Very risky, and the risk was part of the fun. We spent almost every weekend on the beach that summer.

Right after the last Fire Island weekend with Upton in August, Nikos came back from Europe with a bottle of Chanel No. 5 and a bolt of white sari silk. The fabric was spectacular, gossamer thin and shot with gold, with a golden border of arabesques. My love for Nikos was abiding, permanent, not something I could turn off. I loved the way he seemed to delight in my company. When I was being funny, he laughed. When I told him stories, he listened. I felt as though I brought a lightness to his life that he adored and might not otherwise enjoy, and this made me very happy. He paid close attention to what I did and said. I felt like a shining star when I was with Nikos. I felt cherished, and I felt safe. I longed for him to outshine Upton, eclipse him, erase all possibility of Upton in my life. But Upton still swept me into his dangerous, swirling energy; I had to stay alert, ready to jump. In Upton's vortex I was hidden in the shadow of his brilliance, privileged to be so close to his light where anything was possible, seduced by his danger.

I wanted to uproot Upton briefly, put him to the test and bring him to Woods Hole, where I had grown up and where my parents still spent every summer. We would stay with them in their house, where I hoped my darling father's hospitality would offset any rudeness from my mother. We drove up for the long Labor Day weekend, and I could tell before we left New York that Upton was steeling himself for a difficult visit. He had met my parents in New York that spring, and from the start, there was friction between him and my mother. He could tell she disapproved of him even though she never actually called him "lace curtain Irish."

Upton, never one to suffer fools gladly, had his own issues. "Your mother is willfully ignorant," he'd say, disgusted. "I've never known anyone less intellectually curious or more socially ambitious."

I told Upton about her childhood, how her parents had divorced in 1917, when divorce was still taboo and my mother was only five. She was raised in poverty by her saintly and hardworking grandmother, whom I knew as Great-Grandma. Great-Grandma was head of the local chapter of the Woman's Christian Temperance Union and a devout member of the First Congregational Church. She and my great-grandfather, an alcoholic who worked for the Old Colony Railroad, lived on the wrong side of the tracks in Middleboro, Massachusetts, forty miles south of Boston, with his tyrannical and blind mother.

My father came from Middleboro, too, but from very different circumstances. His father and grandfather had sat on the

Governor's Council in Boston, commuting by train from their own private flag stop. When my mother married my father, with his diploma from Exeter Academy and degree from Dartmouth College, the Social Register and all its trappings were suddenly within her reach. But as she climbed up the ladder, rung by rung, she became ever more fearful that she'd be exposed as an imposter, with common roots.

When my mother received us in Woods Hole, already garrulous with bourbon, I doubt she noticed the courteous way Upton unobtrusively clicked his heels when he took her hand, or his slight bow. With a name like Brady, he was doomed from the start. Mummy began by asking Upton about himself, his family, Harvard—her standard way of supposedly making people feel at home. Upton hated it.

"She was grilling me," he said later. "She didn't even listen to my replies! All she did was interrupt."

He was right. His responses weren't nearly as important as her next question. The goal was that she *appear* interested in him.

"It's impossible to exchange an idea with your mother," said Upton, disgusted. "I don't think she's capable of an original idea." I had never looked at my mother from this perspective before.

The weekend was hardly relaxing, except when we went off to the beach, or sailing with my friend Mary, whom Upton knew from New York. My father was a peacemaker and a reader, and would have enjoyed Upton's lively mind if Upton could have relaxed. But it's hard to relax when you are facing the judgment seat, as Upton surely was. We were both glad to get back to New York.

During the week, Upton was off selling books while I went to work, auditions, and dance classes with June Taylor and

Hanya Holm. When summer cooled into fall, we moved to Upton's apartment for steamy weekends, our lovemaking still cut short, still overshadowed by Sunday Mass, only hours away, and limited, too, by my refusal to commit to Upton.

That fall, in the turbulence of aborted sex, or possibly because of it, I experienced the physical miracle of transubstantiation, that moment in the Mass when the priest holds up the wafer of unleavened bread and turns it into flesh, when he raises the silver chalice and transforms wine into blood. I experienced that moment when Christ himself is bodily present; I felt him there in the church as palpable as the bench I kneeled on or the chalice beneath my lips. From then on, the Consecration took on new meaning. This recurring sacrifice of Christ's very body and blood was the visceral power that Upton felt in his loins, a power far more potent than any casual seduction I could offer.

"Making love is for making babies," Upton would say. "That is why it is so sacred."

I believed this, too. When—if—we finally consummated our love, it would be without the intervention of diaphragms or condoms, or the protection of the Pill, hardly available in 1961. We wouldn't make love until we could welcome whatever new life might result. For Upton, this meant no intercourse until I made a commitment to him by ending my relationship with Nikos. For me, the rules were more flexible. I believed that if I could fully commit to either of these two beautiful men in the heat of the moment, that would be commitment enough.

Upton poured himself into his new New York life. In the weeks before he started at Knopf, he improved his apartment, building bookcases and shelves, refinishing tables and chairs he'd rescued from trash trucks, rewiring outlets, hemming old curtains from the house in Portsmouth. He assembled an elegant wardrobe on a shoestring, offsetting the nearly full-price suit from J. Press with Brooks Brothers shirts and Church shoes from Filene's Basement. Before Upton, I had never seen anyone except a tailor reline a tweed jacket, put cuffs on gray flannels, turn a frayed collar on a shirt. He was a whirlwind of proficiency, a Renaissance man, a miracle worker.

He matted and framed a watercolor of a catboat lazily sailing across smooth water that captured the generous essence of all catboats and the drift of tide.

"It's a wonderful painting," I said.

"I worked hard on it. I'm not sure I got the sail exactly right." Upton, squinting, stepped back and studied it from a new angle.

"You painted that?"

"It's our old catboat. The *Lucy.*"

Upton loved having the right tools for the job: Osmiroid pens for calligraphy, barber's shears for trimming hair, a pastry bag and assorted shiny tips for icing cakes or even extruding mashed-potato rosettes. He stocked his tiny kitchenette with carbon steel knives, springform pans, saffron threads, and pine nuts, things I'd never paid any attention to or sometimes never even heard of. When he wanted to buy a rug, we went to a dark storefront on Ninth Avenue, the cavernous inside filled with rolled-up Orientals. In the heavy air, redolent of garlic, curry, and sweet tobacco, Upton discussed the relative merits of Isfehan, Sarouk, and Shiraz rugs with the ancient Persian dealer, both men unrolling rug after dusty rug, while the names spilled off Upton's tongue like church Latin at Mass, or Greek when he quoted Homer. We came home with a very worn but beautiful nine-by-twelve-foot Moud for fifty dollars, and a box of Crayolas bought separately to color in the bald, white patches where the brick-colored wool and jewel-like border had worn away.

My circle of friends expanded that fall as it became *our* circle of friends, widening to include several of Upton's Harvard classmates now working in New York, and new friends as well. One of these was Edward Slocum, who worked on Madison Avenue in advertising. Edward loved women, and women loved Edward. He cared about how we looked, and knew about clothes, hair, makeup, style. He would fuss over me, fingers fluttering.

"Just look at you! So adorable in that little red cape! And the boots! Straight out of the brothers Grimm!"

I was sure Edward was homosexual, and said so to Upton.

"What do mean?" He wheeled on me. "How can you tell?"

"I don't know, there's just something about him . . ."

"Pure conjecture," stated Upton. "You have no idea what you're saying."

But I did have some idea. And I was pretty sure I was right. Not that it mattered, particularly. Edward was Edward—witty, amusing, a bit slick and a name-dropper, and a great spinner of tall tales. Regardless of his sexual preference, which you can be sure I didn't mention again, I liked Edward, and we saw him often for drinks or dinner.

Buff and Upton both decided to go to Portsmouth for the long Columbus Day weekend. Upton asked his mother if I could come, too, and she was delighted, as eager to meet me as I was to meet her. I knew Madee had been widowed six years earlier at age forty-seven, during Upton's senior year at the Priory. Upton's father, diagnosed with inoperable liver cancer in March, was killed by an embolism two weeks afterward, leaving Madee with three children to put through college and no money. And to make matters worse, the Priory made it clear that they expected her to move out of the farmhouse as soon as she could. A week after Upton graduated, they moved to a dreary house across the island, and for the first time in sixteen years there wasn't a single Brady at the Priory. Madee, now faced with having to earn a living, started teaching third grade. She became certified, and five years later was head of the high-school English department. With an inheritance from her father, Madee built a classic three-bedroom Cape overlooking the Sakonnet River. She told Upton she was glad we were all coming so we could help her prune the rosa rugosa hedge and put the garden to bed for the winter.

"Wake up, little Susie, we gotta go home," the Everly Brothers crooned on the radio while Upton and I sped north in the Pontiac. Even though Buff was the one who was officially engaged, and even though I was still seeing Nikos, I sensed that meeting Madee was important, a firsthand glimpse of Brideshead. We arrived in time for the Saturday lunch martini, which always followed the ritual Saturday cleaning.

Madee was the same age as my father and four years older than my mother. She seemed much older than fifty-four to me, and more matronly than I had expected from the photos I'd seen. She was large-boned and moved slowly, so unlike Upton and Buff. Widowhood, or perhaps the exhaustion from raising six children on a shoestring, had aged her prematurely. She gave me an appraising look, her brown eyes smoldering with intelligence. The boys and even Libby had spoken of Madee with a mixture of love and fear, and I was expecting a formidable matriarchal presence when she broke into a lopsided grin, as if inviting me to be her comrade. She opened her arms wide, and I think that intuitively we both knew this would be a deep and permanent friendship, one that would transcend any relationship I might have with Upton. She was the mother I wanted, not my own.

With the martinis came the stories. Right away, she started to create for me, her rapt audience, not just her current world in Portsmouth, with the Priory, the high school, her children, but her childhood in China, her years at Radcliffe, her summer with the University Players—story after story, delivered with operatic drama. She was onstage, just as Upton so often was. Listening to Madee, though he appeared to be spellbound, Upton gave himself away with the occasional rolled eye and raised eyebrow behind her back. Clearly, he had heard many versions of her stories many times, but also, for the first time since I'd known him, Upton was not center stage. Madee was in control of the conversation. And unlike my mother when she met Upton, Madee didn't "grill" me, or even ask the usual polite questions. Instead, she seemed to be getting to know me by my reactions to her stories.

After the martinis, one each and a "dividend," Upton made open-faced toasted cheese and tomato sandwiches, no discussion about it, because this is what Madee always served up for Saturday lunch. And after lunch, the nap, another sacrosanct rite. She was about to retire to her bed with a new book from the Redwood Library when Buff drove up in a noisy, borrowed Volkswagen.

"The muffler fell off on Route 24!" Buff threw up his hands and laughed. "Now what?"

"We'll fix it!" said Upton, and then, turning to Madee, "Got any old orange juice cans?"

In less than an hour, Upton had fashioned a new Minute Maid muffler with two empty cans and some duct tape.

"Let's take it to Purgatory for a test drive," he said, and off we went. Purgatory is a narrow, vertical, and very deep cleft in the high rocky cliff beyond Second Beach. The crevasse is maybe thirty feet wide at its narrowest, and there are stories that span centuries of young men who tried to leap across and fell to their deaths on the rocks below. Upton and Buff raced to the edge, where we leaned over, looking down at the jagged rocks and, beneath them, the boiling surf. Just peering over the edge made me feel sick. The boys took off, sure-footed as a pair of mountain goats, egging each other on like school-yard show-offs.

Suddenly, Upton disappeared under the lip of the cliff. *Oh God, don't let him slip. Don't let him fall.* I could see how easily it would happen; one false step is all it would take. Almost at the bottom, Upton reappeared, and I could breathe again. From the top, he looked now as if he were almost in the surf. I was sure he'd be swept into the surging water. The rocks looked slippery, and Buff had stopped a little higher up, on a flat, dry boulder. I heard him laugh as Upton jumped over the spray. I couldn't watch Upton flirt with disaster another minute and walked away to wait for them in the car.

From the safety of the car, I thought back to a trip I'd taken with Nikos a few years earlier. On a deserted New Hampshire road, Nikos's car spluttered to a stop. We hitchhiked to the nearest gas station, several miles away, where the single attendant said he couldn't possibly leave the station with no one to pump gas while he went off in his truck to tow our car.

"We can pump gas," I said quickly, meaning Nikos could pump gas, something I assumed all men knew how to do. I was dumbfounded to discover that Nikos did not. Fortunately, the attendant came back before any customers appeared.

It was a trivial incident, and yet I'd thought about it a couple of times lately, always shocked by my own impatience with Nikos's ineptitude. Since meeting Upton, I had a new admiration for competence. Maybe I didn't want to live with someone who didn't have his panoply of manual skills. One thing was sure: Nikos never would have scrambled down into Purgatory. He would have stayed with me, his arm protectively around my shoulders, keeping me from straying too close to the lip.

We got back to Madee's in time for drinks, dinner, Scrabble, and more stories. They had such a gift, all of these Bradys, for spinning stories that were so vivid, so immediate, that later, when I remembered them, they became my stories. I wanted to have been there; I wished it had all happened to me. By the time I climbed into Lucy's bed (Lucy, Upton's sister, was a junior at Northfield School in western Massachusetts), I knew I wanted to be a Brady, serving up the mashed potatoes to our six, eight, ten beautiful blond children while at the head of the table, Upton carved the Sunday roast. Maybe, like the days in the Priory farmhouse with Madee and Pa, there wouldn't be much money, but we'd do things ourselves: make our clothes, grow our food, refinish old furniture and even houses, make mufflers out of orange juice cans. We'd be a noisy, curious, vigorous family, probably exhausting but never dull. And we would have our church. Tomorrow I would go to Mass at the Priory and the picture would be complete.

Even though I'd heard stories and seen snapshots, I was not prepared for the sheer beauty of the Priory—the stone walls made of shallow, flat slate that limned the rolling land with such grace, the salt-hazed light on the chapel stones, and the simple crucifix, suspended from radiating gold wires high above the stone altar. I met several monks—Brothers Hilary, Bede, and David—and Father Andrew, all of whom had been important to Madee, Buff, and Upton—but it was Father Andrew I was drawn to. He had shared an office with Upton's father, was his closest friend and a fellow math teacher. I had heard stories about his quicksilver mind and energy and humor, but no one had mentioned the naked compassion that burned from him right to me when he took my hand. I felt he was giving me not just my blessing, but a promise of support that I didn't fully understand.

On our way back to New York on Monday, Upton took a detour to Second Beach in Newport. We got out of the car and walked hand in hand on the hard sand close to the water. After a few minutes he stopped and put his hands on my shoulders.

"I can't live without you," he said, his blue eyes unexpectedly brimming with tears. "I've known since I saw you last winter, maybe since the first dance at the Cotillion."

I stared at his tears, listened to the new tremble in his voice. Upton, the most adept and skillful person I have ever met, thinks he cannot live without me? Surely not.

"I need you." He was almost pleading. "I want to spend my life with you."

"Why didn't you say anything?" I put my hand on his cheek and felt the wetness.

"I was afraid you would turn me away."

"But I love you."

"And Nikos?"

I paused and looked out at the water, shining in the autumn light. "Yes, him, too."

"You have to decide." He pulled me close against him. "I can't go on." And then he said it again. "I cannot live without you."

There was something in his voice that I had never heard before. A frightening desperation, as if he were asking me to save his life, not simply to share it with him.

"Don't worry," I whispered, licking the salt off my lips. "I promise it will be all right." How could I not save someone's life?

A few weeks later, when Upton was scheduled to be selling books in Princeton, Nikos invited me to New Hampshire, where he had just started teaching at a boys' prep school. He was having a little party for all his new faculty friends, and he wanted me to meet them and them to meet me. He reserved a pleasant single room for me at the old inn on the village green. In the last flare of fall, leaves drifted from gnarled maples, and a distant cheer rose from the football field as we walked across the campus to the dorm where Nikos lived in an apartment with a fireplace, leather furniture, and floor-to-ceiling bookshelves. A cluster of pink-cheeked boys outside politely greeted Nikos as Mr. Lambranides and shook my hand, clearly enjoying this whiff of romance.

Nikos planned his party carefully, with good cheeses, nuts, and olives, plenty of ice, plenty of liquor, and even cider. See? I thought. Nikos is not helpless; he is a popular teacher; he knows how to throw a very nice party. Look, he's remembering to fill Mrs. Whatnot's glass. Now he is passing the shrimp. Do not ask what kind of party Upton would have or how he would arrange the furniture. Do not think of Upton. Or mention his name. This is Nikos, the one you have loved for so long. He is showing you a life you could share with him. And I could easily see myself living here as Mrs. Lambranides, newly wed to handsome

Mr. L. I could help the drama coach and serve tea and cider to the boys on rainy afternoons. Make love to Nikos every night, lingering over new pleasures, returning again and again to old ones. But this part of my filmstrip, the lovemaking, was out of focus.

When the party had ended, and Nikos and I were alone together, a sad awkwardness descended. We both said we were tired, and Nikos walked me back to the inn well before midnight, kissed me with a careful tenderness, and left.

In my room, I almost called him. There was still unfinished business. But I didn't know what I wanted to say. Or even what I didn't want to say. I thought of Upton, standing on the beach a week ago, his face wet with tears, saying he could not live without me. I couldn't stop the busy swirl of thoughts, or slow them down enough to sort them out.

The next day, we had lunch with one of Nikos's favorite masters and his wife, a good and pleasant distraction. Then, in the early autumn dusk, Nikos drove me back to Boston and my plane to New York. I was reclining in the bucket seat, my eyes half shut, when I thought I saw a brilliant flash of light on the horizon. A nuclear flash. A bomb. My heart speeded up, and my breathing was shallow. I sat upright and fully opened my eyes.

Nikos turned to me. "What? What is it?"

The horizon was pitch-black, the surrounding countryside peaceful. The few cars on the road were behaving well. There was a moon, and the stars shone the way they do on a clear, cold night. Yet my pulse still raced.

"I don't know. I was just suddenly terrified. For no reason. Terrified."

Nikos nodded gravely, as if this happened every day. "It's a panic attack. Take some deep breaths. Slow, deep breaths."

I did as he told me, and my pulse slowed. "How did you know?"

Nikos tensed, and kept his eyes on the road. "It happened to me all last year. I'd suddenly be overcome with fear. Many nights, I walked all over Cambridge in the cold, until I could breathe again."

That was all he said about it. In the space that followed, I thought about Nikos, fearful and walking in the freezing dark while I danced the merengue in our bright, warm apartment. These were the nights he was thinking about when we talked at Orsini's in June, and all he had said was that the winter had been difficult.

We got to the airport without much time to spare, so our good-bye was hurried. In those days, Logan Airport was one single-story building with a long, flat roof where people often went to wave to departing friends. I trotted across the tarmac, wondering if Nikos was up there waiting for me to turn around and wave. It was all I could do to keep from looking up, but it seemed crucial to stay focused on the plane, on leaving. I climbed up the steps, nearly turning around for a glance at the wind-swept roof before entering the plane. But what if he wasn't there? What if Nikos had had enough of my ambivalence, enough of my not talking about our future? What if his ardor for me had cooled as mine had for him? Head down, I entered the plane. Finally settled in my window seat, I did look back at the terminal building. The roof wasn't lit, but I was sure I saw a tall, lone figure looking toward the plane.

Tears came in a flood. And more adrenaline. My mind raced, my heart raced, as if I were on speed, or teetering on the edge of Purgatory. As soon as we touched down at La Guardia, I took a cab to Penn Station, bought a ticket for the next train to Princeton, and called Upton at the Princeton Inn.

All I said when he picked up the phone was "I've made up my mind, Upton. I'll be there soon."

VERMONT, APRIL 2008

What coat will I wear to the memorial service at Portsmouth Abbey? I root around in the closet and pull out the cape Upton made for me some twenty years ago. I remember him on all fours on the Oriental rug, shears in his hand, cutting the silvery sage-colored wool freehand, in a circle, and then draping it across my shoulders as I stood on the kitchen table.

"Turn around." He twirled his finger, and I turned. "Again, again!" I felt the heavy cloth swirl around me as I spun, as if it had its own energy. "Perfect!" proclaimed Upton.

And it was. With no pattern, he had just made it up, out of whole cloth. When I wear the cape, strangers stop me on the street to ask where it came from, to find out who made such a work of art.

I think back on Upton's talents: he knew how to soothe infant Sarah the day she came home from the hospital, when I had no idea what to do; he played Handel on the recorder, sailed a forty-foot yawl, navigated by the stars. But when someone praised him for his achievements, for my cape, for instance, he would turn the compliment into a criticism.

"Anyone," he would say in almost a sneer, "can learn to sew."

In other words, Upton would have you believe that it wasn't that he was gifted, it was that the rest of us were dolts. I had tried to learn to sew, hoping Upton would help. But my clumsiness drove him crazy, and instead of teaching me, he would end up ripping out my crooked seam or untangling the wayward thread. His brilliant expertise could make me feel inadequate, but it also seduced me, made me want to marry him, bear his children, spend my life with him.

I look at the little fan Upton installed a month before he

died, to pull hot air from the woodstove downstairs up to his chilly office. It had taken him hours to put it up, it was so exhausting to work with his hands over his head, and he'd had to take many breaks, sitting down and breathing hard. But the fan is correctly in place, the cord invisible, secured by staples to the door frame. Did he know how much I admired the scope of his talents and interests? How I respected his aversion to a sloppy job? Probably not. It was hard to talk to Upton from the heart. He avoided displays of emotion; they were treacherous, unpredictable. No wonder he became skilled at controlling how we all behaved. Every day I think of things I didn't dare to say or do, things I long to tell him now. I remember a line from Yeats:

> *I have spread my dreams under your feet;*
> *Tread softly because you tread on my dreams.*

I see Upton at twenty-three, so full of life and promise. I see him at forty-three and even a month ago, almost seventy, still nourished daily by new ideas and new skills. When he was alive, I was not aware that he ever spread his dreams under my feet, but now, thinking back, I believe he did so nearly every day. The dreams weren't obvious to me; they came disguised as stories, or quotations, a beautiful painting of nasturtiums by Bonnard, a Bach chorale, a meticulously installed fan. How many times, I wonder, did I unknowingly tread on them?

Outside on the Abbey flagstones, I pause, breathing in the salty air from Narragansett Bay before going inside the chapel to send Upton on his way. Suddenly, I twirl, for Upton, and twirl again, again! and feel the cape ripple outward before it settles around my legs.

Upton and Sally.
New York, 1962.

3

*Passion might arise unbidden, but love
is a discipline.*

—JULIA ALVAREZ

WOODS HOLE, APRIL 2008

When I called the children to tell them about Upton, saying tearfully that I had very bad news, each of them immediately thought I was calling about my ninety-six-year-old mother. I still feel angry that she is alive and Upton isn't, and then guilty for feeling this way. She is mentally alert, as sharp as ever, and physically comfortable, but very unhappy in the nursing home, where she has no control over her life. She complains about the food and how long it takes the nurses to answer her call button. She is obsessed with the other residents, whom she observes critically from her chair as they have lunch in the dayroom across the hall but with whom she does not want any contact whatsoever. She doesn't enjoy the beautiful view of the water, or the visits from her grandchildren and great-grandchildren, or from her daughters, Joan and me. I can understand all this. But right now, standing beside her chair, I don't have much patience for it.

I wonder how much longer it will be before we have another memorial service. Mummy knows Upton has died but barely looks at the flowers I put on her table from his service yesterday at the Abbey. I tell her the people she knows who came. She nods, her eyes on the activity in the dayroom. I tell her about Alex's and Sarah's moving memories of Upton, and the beautifully sung Mozart Alleluia. I tell her about her great-grandchildren climbing the tree outside the chapel. Again she nods, eyes still across the hall.

"Look! That one can't get her walker through the door!"

I follow her crooked arthritic finger and see a woman working hard to maneuver her walker into the dayroom. A sob wells up in my throat. Why can't my mother pay attention to me?

For the past two and a half weeks, I have been mothering my children and grandchildren, and my children have been right beside me, helping with the daily business of living, and the business of grieving, too. I know they would take care of me if I needed them to. But I'm okay. Nonetheless, just for a moment, I would like my mother to mother me. I would like her simply to acknowledge what I'm going through. I think of the attentive, loving care Sarah and my daughters-in-law bestow on my grandchildren. Tracy is almost eight months pregnant. During Upton's service, fifteen-month-old Ryder nestled into the little that is left of Tracy's lap, his silky blond head resting on her breast, her hand stroking his cheek. That is what I would like to do; climb up for just for a minute, feel a cool hand on my hot cheek.

I put my hand on Mummy's bony shoulder. "I have to catch the bus."

It's a five-hour trip home to Vermont. Andrew, Mari, four-year-old Nina, and two-year-old Aki will all be arriving for supper.

They are the last of the children to leave, and will be in Vermont another two days before they fly back to San Francisco. It's good the way my children have been returning to their lives one by one. A total exodus would have been hard to weather, but now it's time for them all to go.

I lean over to kiss my mother's dry cheek.

"Well," she says, finally looking at me. "It's nice Upton will be there to welcome you when you get home."

Her words hang in the overheated nursing home air. I freeze, caught by her rigid smile.

I take a deep breath. "Upton is dead."

For a few seconds more, she keeps on smiling, unable to switch gears. I know she didn't mean to say that. I know she didn't think about what she was saying, that it was an automatic response to my saying good-bye. But this makes me even more furious. All her life my mother has said what she wanted to say, without really thinking about the effect of her words on other people. She has often relied on pat responses, like this one about Upton's being there when I get home. And we've all let her get away with it.

Now I am stony. "Upton is dead." I say it once more, watching the smile fade on her bright, stubborn little face. "Upton will never welcome me home again."

This time, the words sink in. "I know." She looks embarrassed, and I leave fast.

NEW YORK, 1962

After that first spangled night of consummated love with Upton, I came downstairs with a new pride and a shyness, too, wondering if the world would instantly recognize that I was no longer a virgin. Now that it had finally happened, I could hardly think of anything else, and the weeknights when Upton was on the road seemed empty and cheerless. I bought expensive bath oils and lotions, and even a slim can of spermicidal foam, a minimal precaution against getting pregnant that I didn't mention to Upton. He was still bothered by premarital sex, and I was often the one who insisted we give in to our passion. He was eager to become properly engaged, and the first step was for him to formally ask my father for my hand in marriage. We both came to Cambridge shortly after New Year's.

My mother and I stayed in the kitchen, leaving the men to talk before we all settled down for cocktails. I heard Upton clear his throat and call my father "sir" as the kitchen door swung shut. My mother gave me a narrow look and bristled as she put cheese and crackers on a plate, "blotting paper," she called it, for the cocktails. Neither one of us mentioned what was going on in the living room.

Later that night when we were alone, Upton told me that my father had been gracious when they'd talked, clearly wanting to put Upton at ease.

"If Sally wants to marry you, I will be delighted to give you her hand." He offered Upton his own hand and they shook on it. But then my father added, "Unfortunately, I can't speak for Mrs. Ryder."

I watched Upton grind out his cigarette. "Why did he have to say that? I wasn't asking for *her* permission."

"Lucky you weren't!"

Upton shot me a disdainful look. "Does your father ever stand up to her?"

"What do you mean?"

"He's so *weak*."

I thought about all the times I'd heard Mummy rip into my father, criticize him for his lack of ambition, strip him of his dignity.

"You should have told Mr. X you were the *associate director* of the Oceanographic," she'd say, "not just that you *worked* there!"

Or "Why didn't you say you went to school with *Nelson Rockefeller* and the *Haffenreffers*?"

I had watched her undercut him over and over again. But I saw my father not as weak but as the peacemaker, quiet, just, and sane, even in the wake of my mother's frequent self-absorbed frenzies. My mother was used to getting her own way. Not one of us wanted to confront her and risk unleashing her rampant, irrational fury. I tried to explain this to Upton, but his mind was made up: My father was weak, my mother was against our marriage, and he, Upton, couldn't live without me.

His mother, on the other hand, was ecstatic, and like everyone else (except my mother) wanted to know when the wedding would take place. I hedged. I was beginning to get callbacks for auditions, two agents were mildly interested in representing me, and I wanted to give my acting career one last push before I got married and had babies. When Upton prodded me to come up with a date, I told him we would marry in the fall. I still hadn't said anything to Nikos about my marrying Upton. I knew this wasn't fair, but I couldn't bear to end it, to lose him from my life. Nikos and I hadn't seen each other since the weekend in New Hampshire. There had been phone calls and gentle letters, that's all. I missed his quiet humor, his respectful pleasure in my company. And I thought about him often, never completely giving up my old vision of our future together. But I was going to marry Upton.

Pat, Lib's replacement, and I still lived in the apartment, but on the weekends when Upton was in the city, I usually stayed with him. When he was sober, he was a tender and ardent lover, but sometimes before and even during sex, there was a shadow, like a papal frown. Until we were married, Upton would never be entirely comfortable having sex. There was something old-fashioned and upright about this that I admired.

Upton had grown up with Kipling's Just So Stories, and his conversation was laced with Kipling quotes that I didn't recognize: "the great grey-green greasy Limpopo River all set about with fever-trees," for instance, or the Elephant Child with his "'satiable curtiosity." Upton presented me with a beautiful edition of the Just So Stories, inscribed in his Chancery hand to *My Best Beloved*. I soon learned that most of the stories invoke the Best Beloved, and we began to call each other that, in private whispers.

We kept on dancing, but without Buff and Lib, there was something missing when we danced in the apartment. When we could afford it, we'd go to the Rendezvous Room at the Plaza or to one of the local bars on Eighty-sixth Street where people danced to the jukebox. Dancing was more intense, more intimate, in public. Someday, I knew Upton would bring me to

Saint Thomas, take me to The Gate, where he first danced the merengue. I could almost feel the damp air on my neck.

In March, I auditioned for the Greenville Playhouse in the Catskills, and was hired as leading lady. It was a non-Equity summer stock company, and the pay, even for leading lady, was terrible. But I wanted to do it, and wanted this experience on my résumé. I quit my job in Manhattan and couldn't afford to keep the apartment over the summer while I was away, especially since Pat was leaving, too. But Upton's sublet on Ninety-second Street conveniently ended July 1, so he took over my lease and moved in while I was in the Catskills. This meant I didn't have to move out or pay rent, a perfect solution. Upton had most of the summer off from Knopf and would be teaching Latin at the Priory summer school in July. And in the fall? Well, we were getting married. We could work out all the details later, after the show was over.

The Greenville Playhouse was not in the strawhat circuit, or even the borscht belt. The tiny white clapboard theater stood on tree-lined Main Street in Greenville, New York, a Rip van Winkle backwater on the edge of the Catskills. A young woman from Albany with more money than theater experience owned the theater and dreamed of turning it into a little jewel. This was her first summer.

There were eight actors in the company, plus two lazy apprentices, two set/costume designers, a lighting technician, a manager, and a director. We performed one show at night and rehearsed two others during the day; six weeks of shows. The dressing rooms were under the theater in a damp cellar with a dirt floor, the men's and women's areas separated by a sagging curtain strung on a clothesline. To get from the dressing room to the stage, we had to go outdoors and up a dirt path to the side door of the theater. When it rained, the path turned to mud, as did our makeup if we weren't careful. Upton couldn't come until August, when summer school was over, but he sent care packages with books, Roger & Gallet carnation soap, tins of homemade cookies, and once, a loaf of his bread, which I brought to the dressing room to share with everyone. When I came down at intermission to change my costume I found a large rat tearing at the bread with his claws, his eyes yellow in the glare of the naked lightbulb.

The Moon Is Blue was the final production and ran the first two weeks in August. This classic romantic comedy was made for summer stock and was easy for me because I'd performed it three years earlier in Cambridge, with Nikos as the romantic leading man. This time as Patty O'Neill, I had a new leading man. Just as I did as Sally Ryder.

Upton arrived in Greenville two days before we opened, right after the set designer and his partner stormed off, leaving us with no Act One and Act Three set of Manhattan, as seen from the top of the Empire State Building at dusk. It's an important set, which inspires many lines about the view.

"I can paint the backdrop," said Upton. "No problem."

And he did. The set was stunning, the paint still damp in places when the curtain went up. The only problem, which I couldn't bring myself to tell him, was that in Act One, it was supposed to be foggy, and the view impaired. Upton's skyline was brilliant, lights bright in the mountain range of skyscrapers. I knew there wasn't time to rig a scrim, but I wasn't prepared for the laughter that erupted after my line about the fog ruining the view. Upton was crushed.

"Why didn't you tell me? I feel like a fool."

I had no real excuse except that it was opening night for me, and I wasn't thinking about Upton or the set.

I don't think he ever really forgave me for that. It was a skillful, professional set and he'd dashed it off so generously. I don't think I've ever forgiven myself, either—it would have been so easy for me to have told him about the fog, and spared him humiliation.

After the show, we went to the local bar for burgers and beer, and danced to "Midnight in Moscow" and "The Stripper" on the jukebox before sneaking into Upton's bed at the local inn. The upright Christian family who owned the inn had been wary of us "theater people" since we'd arrived. But with only two weeks to go, I didn't care, and besides, it had been nearly two months since Upton and I had been together. He hadn't gotten drunk, and he was as hungry as I. Our bodies finally quiet, and still fitting together as if cast from the same mold, we watched the sky lighten. His fingers wandered like wings of a moth across my forehead, my cheeks, my neck while I breathed in his smell— fresh and sweet and mildly astringent.

"So when will we do it?" he asked. "Labor Day?"

"That's only a month!" I remembered my mother's frenzy five years ago when my sister got married, also on Labor Day weekend, with not quite a month's notice.

"It doesn't have to be a big wedding." Upton's hand moved to my shoulder, his fingers firm now. "I don't want a big wedding, do you?"

I shook my head, remembering the headlines in the local paper after my sister's extravaganza: "Four Hundred See Joan Ryder Wed!"

I was pretty sure my mother would want to keep this wedding small. After all, I was marrying an Irish Catholic, not a Social Register blue blood.

"What about Columbus Day weekend in Woods Hole?" This would give my mother enough time and the guests an extra day to travel, and the weather was usually beautiful on the Cape in early October.

"I guess I can wait until then." His fingers began their traceries on my face again and I settled my head into the hollow of his smooth shoulder.

On Sunday, Upton left Greenville, and the next Friday, Nikos arrived. I was waiting for him at the inn, and felt the old rush of pleasure when the little Alfa Romeo pulled up. He climbed out of the car and took me in his arms, a good, safe, familiar place to be, and then he kissed me. I expected another stronger rush of emotion when our lips met, searched for it, but it wasn't there. Did Nikos feel the loss, too? How could I be thinking this way when I was about to marry Upton? I had to tell Nikos; I wasn't being fair. But not now. I had a show to do. The innkeeper gave him Upton's same room, but this time I didn't go in.

It was odd appearing as Patty O'Neill in *The Moon Is Blue* knowing Nikos was in the audience watching me instead of onstage playing opposite me. What was it like for him, seeing me in the same role and someone else in his? There was a dark mirroring of life that I hadn't foreseen. After the show we went to the bar for beer and burgers—it was the only place to eat in Greenville after ten at night—but this time, I didn't dance to the jukebox. We sat at a table in the back, a perfect place for me to tell him it was over and I was going to marry Upton, but I just couldn't say the words. When I first dated Nikos, I was barely seventeen. Now I was twenty-two. I'd loved him for almost a fifth of my life. And even though what I once believed was a very rare, huge, and permanent passion had slipped away, I hung on to that old vision of us together, married, comfortable, and safe. The fire had cooled, but the love was still there, and I clung to it.

As soon as Nikos left on Sunday for New York, I called my parents. My mother actually sounded excited when I told her I wanted to be married in Woods Hole on Columbus Day weekend.

"A small wedding, Mummy. Nothing fancy."

"Well! Good thing I've saved the lists from Joan's wedding." I could hear the wedding engine rumbling to life.

The next weekend, we struck the set and closed the theater, and my mother drove to Greenville, to bring me back to Woods Hole. As soon as I was in the car with her, I was catapulted into the crazy cosmos of The Wedding. She'd already called the caterer, who'd come down from Boston to check out the grounds for tents. There were menus waiting for me to look at, and sample invitations. The reception was clearly the star, with maybe a supporting role for the bride. There was no mention of the groom. It was almost as if Mummy had forgotten that I was marrying the wrong person. I hoped her oblivion would last as long as possible.

The wheels were in motion, and I could feel them pick up speed.

On the way home, we passed a sign on the Mass Pike for the town of Upton.

"Hey!" I said to Mummy. "Why don't we drive through Upton?" This was risky; just mentioning his name might make her bristle. But she laughed.

"Why not?"

We turned off the Pike and soon found ourselves in a poor-looking town, with empty, treeless streets and a few derelict brick mill buildings with broken windows and old newspapers swirling on the dusty ground. Such a nice name, Upton; but such a sad town. Mummy drove right through without making a single snide remark about what a blue-collar place Upton was. For the moment, she was happy to be with me, happy to be making plans. But with Mummy, I never knew when her mood might change.

I had barely unpacked when she announced that she was writing to Madee. "This is what the mother of the bride does," she said. "I'm inviting her to dinner. With Upton."

That sounded like a good plan. They ought to finally meet, discuss wedding plans, exchange lists. My mother fluttered with lists—for the caterer, the florist, the photographer. I began to see that this was her wedding. Well, maybe that would be okay, though I hoped it wouldn't get too fancy. For now at least, her focus was on planning everything, and not on the Catholic part. All I wanted was to be married by Father Andrew, and surrounded by the people I loved. I hoped there would be beautiful music, good simple food, some wine. No limos, no bridesmaids (except my sister), no presents on display, no waiters in black and white. But by now my mother was in high gear. Whatever she did, there would be no turning back. Or so I thought.

I finally sat down and wrote to Nikos. I couldn't put it off any longer. I didn't know what to say—surely not that I would always love him; no, not that. I felt like apologizing, but for what? "I wanted to let you know that Upton and I will be getting married in Woods Hole on October 13 . . ." It was a short letter, yet it took me several teary tries to finally come up with a clean copy. Nikos answered by return mail, politely wishing me well. I didn't expect such a pervasive feeling of loss to sweep through me, leaving a sadness that bloomed in secret, and only when I was alone.

A few days before Upton and Madee came to dinner, my mother announced that she just couldn't reconcile herself to a Catholic wedding, in a Catholic church.

"Are you sure you can't get permission to have the wedding in the Church of the Messiah?" asked Mummy one more time.

The Church of the Messiah is a classic Episcopal church with ivy-covered stones and an herb garden. I sang in the choir from fifth grade on, and saw the steeple from my bedroom window. My father was a vestryman, my sister was married there, though the church was too small to hold all four hundred guests.

"Or what about right here?" Mummy gestured toward the garden at the end of the wide lawn. "Overlooking the water."

I explained once again that the Catholic Church demanded that the ceremony take place on consecrated ground.

She sighed. "I just don't have any relationship with St. Joseph's."

St. Joseph's is the wooden Roman Catholic church, very blue-collar, with pastel Marys and Stations of the Cross on the walls, and over the altar, a crucifix with blood dribbling from the crown of thorns and the nail holes. The best feature of St. Joe's is the bell tower, right across the street. The gift of a wealthy parishioner, the bell tower is a simple campanile made of pale peach–colored stone. It stands at the base of a long, narrow garden, buffered from the street by a tall hedge, and partly open to the water on the other side. The small, sweet bell rings the Angelus three times a day, at six in the morning, at noon, and at six in the evening, each time pealing three sets of three bells with a pause between each set. Then the deep, big bell strikes the hour, six or twelve.

The bell tower is right on the edge of Eel Pond, a large tidal pond in the middle of the village, and the bells can be heard all over town. When I was growing up in Woods Hole, the bells told me when to get up, when to come home for lunch, and when to come home for dinner. I wondered if maybe the bell tower ground was sanctified. I called Upton.

"I know Cardinal Cushing from the Harvard Catholic Club. I'll write him and ask."

We were still waiting for the cardinal's reply when Upton and his mother drove over from Portsmouth for dinner. For my mother, there was still hope that she could avoid St. Joseph's. However, time was growing short. Everyone, from the engraver to the bride and groom, was waiting to find out from her where the marriage would take place.

All of us were on our best behavior that night. We sipped cocktails on the terrace watching Madee and my mother, both falsely polite, spar over who was the greater lady, with the more impressive connections. My father made sure everyone's glass was full, and Upton and I tried not to roll our eyes.

Madee gave my mother a list of people to be invited, with addresses, and my mother made sweeping gestures across the lawn where the tent with its water view would be. They talked about finger sandwiches, and champagne. And then my mother hauled out the large leather album of pictures from my sister's wedding.

By this time, everyone had had too much to drink, and there was no sign of dinner. Upton and I went to the kitchen and started heating things up. My mother did have everything ready, just not finished. Finally, we ate. I don't remember anything except relief when it was finally over.

A few days later, Upton heard from the cardinal, who said he was truly sorry, but the bell tower garden was not an option. I dreaded telling my mother. All her life, she expected to get her own way, and because she could be so unpleasant, even frightening, when she didn't, we never crossed her. I decided to tell her after dinner, thinking the news might go down more easily after a few glasses of Jim Beam. We were in the kitchen. I was on one side of the island, wrapping up leftovers, and she was on the other, unloading silverware from the dishwasher.

I took a deep breath. "The cardinal says we have to get married in St. Joseph's." For a moment, my mother froze.

Suddenly, forks and spoons flew at me across the island. When my mother's hand was empty, she stormed out of the kitchen, two bright spots on her cheeks, her eyes brimming.

The next day, she was as calm as ice. "I've given this a great deal of thought," she said, "and I simply cannot go to that church. My only connection to St. Joseph's is taking the help there on Sundays."

The help? What help? What was she talking about? We didn't have servants. And then I remembered one summer at least eight years ago when we had a cook for the month of August. She was from the Azores. And she was Catholic. That's it. Not counting the cleaning lady who came once a week, also Portuguese, but she didn't live with us, and my mother never took her anywhere.

"Of course"—she gave me one of her bright little smiles—"I'll

be at the reception, I'll send out the invitations, I'll do everything. I just won't go to the church."

I couldn't believe what I'd heard. My mother would not
witness my marriage. What could I do?

I called Upton.

"Let me get this straight," he said. "Your mother is not
coming to the church?"

'That's right." There was a pause.

I didn't realize Madee was right there next to Upton until I
heard her say in a loud fury, "If Dotty Ryder won't come to the
church, I'll be goddamned if I'll go to her party afterward."

"Does she mean that?" I asked.

"I think so," said Upton.

"So my mother won't come to the church, and your mother
won't come to the reception, right?"

"Right."

"Okay, well, I'll call you back in a minute. I need to think."

It didn't take me long to realize that this whole wedding was
a huge mistake. My mother's fit the night before with the silverware was one thing. Her not coming to the church was quite another. And now Madee would not come to the reception. This
was my wedding, a celebration of love, not hate. I called Upton
back and told him the wedding was off.

"They've poisoned it. This is all wrong."

"But I want to marry you." Upton sounded desperate.

"We can do it later. But right now I'm calling it off."

"I'm coming over." Upton hung up the phone.

It was a chilly day, a harbinger of fall, and by the time the
solid-gold Pontiac rolled into the driveway, it had started to
drizzle. My mother had been hovering ever since the phone calls,

and I certainly wasn't going to talk to Upton with her around. We drove down the hill to the beach, Upton looking pale and shaky. When we got out of the car, I took his hand.

"It's okay. We'll still get married. Just not now."

"No," said Upton, tight-lipped. "No. Either you marry me now, or I never want to see you again."

"What? You can't wait a couple of months?"

He looked rigid. Miserable. "No. It's now or the marriage is off."

"All I need is to get away from these women. All I need is time. Is that so hard?"

I waited for him to take me in his arms, to comfort me, to be my ally in the face of our mean mothers, but Upton just stood there by the water's edge, his face wet with rain and tears, shaking his head. Where was the man who couldn't live without me?

"It's only a month or two," I said. "Come on!"

"Sally." His voice broke on my name. "It's now or not at all."

There was something familiar in Upton's behavior, a little like my own willful mother's; a little like his. A warning sign. Maybe I didn't want to marry him after all.

"Okay," I said. "Then don't wait. Leave. The marriage is off."

So Upton returned to Portsmouth and then to New York, where he had happily moved into what was formerly *my* apartment; my mother canceled the wedding invitations and the caterer; and I sat down and wrote to Nikos. "I have just called off the wedding, and I wanted you to know . . ." Another short letter, and another polite reply, this one inviting me to let him know if I came to New York.

It soon dawned on me that I was stuck. I'd left my job in New York to go to the Greenville Playhouse, I'd given my apartment to Upton, and expecting to return in the fall, I'd also left all my warm clothes there. So I had no place to live and no job, and soon I would have no clothes. I took a long walk with my good friend Kitty Bacon, eleven years older than I, married with six small children and living a few houses away in Woods Hole. I told her the whole messy story.

"Poor darling! Are you heartbroken?"

She was the first person to ask me that. I thought carefully before I answered.

"No. I'm furious. I just want to get away from them all. From my mother. From Upton's mother. From him!" And I burst into tears.

"I know just what you should do!" Her green eyes were full of light. "Go to Paris! I can find you a place to stay, and I know people who could probably find you a job."

Paris! Kitty made it feel like a fait accompli. She and her husband had lived in Paris for years; she did know many people and has always had a gift for putting them together. Maybe I could do this. Make a brand-new life. Forget Upton.

I decided to go to New York, stay with Joan and Peter, and get my clothes and other things from the apartment. Then start the Paris plan. In the meantime, I wrote Nikos another short note, saying I'd be in New York October 7 for a few days. He answered right away, said he'd love to see me, and invited me to have dinner with him on October 8. I felt a ripple of excitement. Maybe Nikos and I could start again. I also let Upton know that I was coming down, and asked him if he could arrange to be away from the apartment on October 15 from twelve to two so I could get my clothes. He, too, answered promptly:

Dear Sally, The apartment will be empty all day on October 15. Come whenever you like to get your things. Upton." There was a finality to his note, written in his graceful hand, that announced a looming loss. Yet I also was eager to see Nikos, this time without Upton shimmering behind my eyes. And there was Paris—a new life with new people, new possibilities. I was moving on.

A friend in New York had invited me to a party she was giving on Sunday, October 14, and I accepted, thinking a big party might be good for chasing away the demons. I hadn't been there long when I spotted Upton at the bar, talking with our hostess. It was the long Columbus Day weekend, the very weekend of our now-canceled wedding, and I assumed he'd be in Portsmouth. But here we both were. For a half hour or so, we each tried to pretend the other wasn't there, while furtively searching the chattering crowd to make sure he/she was. At one point, our eyes locked across the room, and Upton walked very deliberately through all the other guests to me.

"Come on," he said. "Let's get out of here."

Back at the apartment, each of us feeling vulnerable, we thrashed out the nastiness of the mothers, and Upton's insistence that we marry or we break up, and my anger that Upton had refused to wait until the dust had settled before we made another plan to marry. Throughout this long, tear-filled night, Upton said repeatedly that he could not live without me.

"Upton. Upton, I am going to live with you. Marry you. I promise." I said this many times that night.

It didn't matter. Upton was convinced I was canceling our marriage for good. And he was terrified, that was plain. I didn't know what exactly he was afraid of; I had no idea of the root of his encompassing fear, only that the fear itself was palpable. October 14 was a very long night, full of every kind of tears—rage, sorrow, happiness—and it ended in bed (one bed, no precautions) as the sky turned from black to gray. But only after I had agreed to go to St. Thomas More church as soon as the office was open. We would talk to the pastor and make a date for our marriage.

Previously a Dutch Reform church, St. Thomas More looks more Protestant than Catholic. No tasteless tortured Christs or pastel Virgins here. I thought that maybe even my mother might approve. After we met with the priest and reserved the Lady Chapel for November 17, we were kneeling for a moment on the way out when a rich flood of organ music suddenly rolled over us: Purcell, Vivaldi, the very kind of music we both wanted at our wedding. As soon as the organist took a break, Upton introduced himself. The organist turned out to be Kalman Antos, a well-known composer and teacher. Upton asked him to play at our wedding, Antos checked his calendar and said he'd be delighted, and Upton whipped out his checkbook. This time, it was really going to happen.

Back at the apartment, I called my father, asking him to please come to New York that November weekend and give me away.

"You can count on me," he said. "Of course I will be there." Then he paused. "But I can't speak for your mother."

My mother spoke for herself an hour later, and said she would not be there.

I told Upton.

"All women are impossible after they turn forty," he said, as if this were a commonly accepted truth.

"What on earth do you mean?" This was crazy!

"When Madee turned forty, she kicked Pa out of the bedroom," said Upton, disgust seeping from his words. "From then on, he slept in his study under the stairs."

"Why?" Something terrible must have happened between them for this to occur.

Upton shrugged. "She just did. She would take to her bed— migraines, she said. In the morning she'd come downstairs with a 'Guess what I'm angry about today' look on her face."

"But Upton," I said, slowly. "I am not your mother. Or my mother."

He shrugged again, *another shrug,* as if to say, *Just wait and see,* and then he walked away.

Maybe I should have reminded him that I was the one he said he could not live without. Maybe I should have said firmly that I had no intention of becoming impossible when I hit forty. But Upton had turned his back. This conversation was over.

Back at Joan's, I had two hurdles. First, she was very upset that I'd spent the night with Upton. I told her it was important, that we'd had a lot of hard issues to work through. Then I told her we'd gone to church, talked with a priest, and set the date. This news helped. I asked her to be my matron of honor, and told her Buff would be Upton's best man. I told her I'd talked with Daddy, and he said he would certainly be there to give me away. All of this mollified her somewhat, but it didn't eradicate the stain of my having spent the night with my intended. Joan had no idea how many nights I'd already spent in Upton's bed.

"When Mummy finds out, she'll have a complete break- down. You will have driven her to that."

"Finds out? Why would she find out?" I couldn't believe that Joan would tell her. "And if she has a breakdown, she has a break- down. I'm not responsible for her mental health!"

But Joanie truly believed I would be responsible if my mother fell apart. Joan is four years older than I, and has always been the good girl, the one who knuckled under and did as she was told. I've always been the rebel. And our mother has always been more willful and persevering than either of her daughters, even before she turned forty! I knew there wasn't any chance of Mummy's falling apart. Joan disagreed, and made me promise to spend every night until November 17 at her apartment.

The second hurdle was Nikos. I called him to say that the wedding was on again, and to cancel our date for dinner.

"I'm glad you worked out your wedding plans. But tonight, we have a date." I'd never heard Nikos be so stern. "I'll pick you up at seven."

We went to the apartment he'd recently taken on Riverside Drive with two friends from Harvard whom I knew very slightly. They, too, had dates, and after a drink, we all squeezed into someone's car—I had to perch on Nikos's lap—and drove off to a party. Nikos did not put his arms around me while the car lurched through Central Park. He barely met my eyes when I turned around to look at him, and when he did meet my eyes, he looked removed. At first I tried to be cheerful and think of amusing things to say while balancing on his knees, but nothing I said or did felt right. It was a miserable evening, and a sour way to part. It felt like a punishment, something I probably deserved.

I got my old job back right away and told Kitty I wouldn't be going to Paris after all. Upton and I called our closest friends and told them the wedding was on.

"This time it will be the way we want it, with everyone coming back here afterward to celebrate."

My good friend Mary lived in the apartment below ours, and we planned to have the reception on both floors, with the doors wide open. Practically everyone we called offered to bring something to eat. Buff invited the wedding party—Joan, Peter, my father, Madee, Upton, and me—to our apartment for paella for the night before the wedding. Everything was finally going to be just the way we wanted it.

I went to my friend Milton, a designer with a small boutique on Madison Avenue. I'd done a little modeling for him a couple of times, and the year before he had designed two beautiful dresses for me.

He pulled out a bolt of oyster silk brocade. "Simple and elegant. High neck, long sleeves with a hint of leg-o'-mutton, narrow skirt full enough for dancing, maybe a slit in the back—what do you think?"

When Milton found out I was paying for my wedding dress myself (in 1962, most young brides did not), he charged me $50; a very reasonable price even though prices were different back then. (My apartment was $150 a month, and today it rents for over $2,500.)

I had several fittings for the dress, and was surprised each time how tight the bodice was. At every fitting, Milton let out the darts a little more, and the dress would still be tight the following week. And then my period was late.

I told Upton I thought I might be pregnant.

"Oh, sweetheart!" His eyes were shiny with tears. "I am so happy!"

"It must have been that one night before we went to St. Thomas More."

"Which makes it perfect!"

That night, Upton invited me to the Carlyle for a drink, something I knew he really couldn't afford. We raised our glasses to each other and to the baby, and then Upton took a dark domed velvet box from his pocket. Inside, a cabochon emerald, small but brightly veined (*grassy,* Upton called it), glowed against the ivory satin, flanked by two sparkling diamond chips. It was my engagement ring, and as much of a surprise as the new life we also celebrated that night.

We didn't tell anyone about the baby, and I didn't go to the doctor. That could wait until after we were married. For now, it was our delicious secret. I thought of the baby when I looked at my ring, and when other people looked at it, too. The visible ring, and the secret baby.

Less than two weeks before the wedding, my mother called. She had decided she would "be able" to come after all. Not only that, she wanted to "help" with the wedding plans. She wanted to "do the right thing." This did not mean she'd had a change of heart and now sanctioned this marriage. Doing "the right thing" meant following all the accepted forms of getting married: hiring a limo and a photographer, getting engraved announcements sent out the day before, and presumably, attending the wedding itself. "Helping" meant replacing our lovely, informal post-wedding party with a strained and formal reception at Joan and Peter's for only the eleven members of the immediate family and no one else. Not even Madee's sister was invited, and Buff, as best man, was the only one of Upton's five siblings who was allowed to come. My sister ordered a beautiful little cake and perfect finger sandwiches, and my father provided champagne. I simply went along with all this, exhausted and still raw from the previous pre-wedding scenes in Woods Hole. Now getting married was just something that needed to be done. A sacrament no matter how many people came for the cake.

The morning of the wedding, Upton and I met Father Andrew at the church for a private Mass. Because I was not a Catholic, I could not receive the sacraments, but Father Andrew invited me to the altar rail and gave me my own blessing as I knelt beside Upton. I felt tears well up, and then these unbidden, unspoken words thundered through my head: "Dear God, help me make this marriage work. Please help me make it work."

I was supposed to be radiant, full of joy and hope, confident in a future with my beloved. Where had this fear of failure come from? Who would get married already knowing she would need divine help to make the marriage work? This scared me. Somewhere, in some hidden well deep inside, was an impenetrable darkness.

That afternoon at three, the Lady Chapel at St. Thomas More was filled, and as one of our friends said later, "There wasn't a dry eye in the house." My dress was gorgeous and not too snug. I wore my sister's heirloom veil and, on my right hand, a large sapphire and diamond ring that Peter slipped on my finger on the way to the church.

"It's a family ring," he said. "For you to wear when you make your vows. For luck."

After the ceremony, with the final strains of Purcell still pouring from the organ, Upton and I stood on the steps of the church greeting our friends in the November chill, while the limo purred at the curb and my mother looked at her watch. Finally, the limo took her and my father back to Joan and Peter's, so Upton and I could have a few more minutes with our well-wishers, since they weren't invited to the reception. It was awkward for us all, and hard not to be angry with my mother. The limo returned and we climbed in, hoping that everyone else would go to Mary's and celebrate without us.

The proper reception was just that, proper. And short. My mother was civil to Upton and his mother, and to me, but any outpouring of love was replaced by melodrama. At my wedding, Mummy played the victim, a well-rehearsed role and one my father and Joan and I were practiced at covering up. But I think everyone was relieved when I appeared in my "traveling dress" and Upton and I hopped into the limo for one last ride, this time down Fifth Avenue to the Plaza Hotel. A very kind and to this day anonymous benefactor had changed Upton's reservation from one room with a double bed to a very fancy suite. A fire crackled in the parlor, where a bottle of Dom Pérignon waited in ice, and in the bedroom, a big double bed looked out on the Paris Theatre cinema, whose marquee announced *Divorce Italian Style*, which made us both laugh.

Our honeymoon was a single, tender night of laughter, passion, and simple trust. At least that is how it seems to me now, forty-six years later. I remember thinking as we lay together, full and exhausted, what trust it took to surrender your body to someone else, to lie beside him unconscious, night after night, for the rest of your life.

The next morning, we walked to St. Patrick's Cathedral for Sunday Mass. The enormous church was full, the air thick with layers of incense, the choir and clergy costumed in scarlet, lace, and opulent gold brocade. Cardinal Spellman in his miter, crosier at his side, sang the Mass in Latin, the words by now familiar even to me, the non-Catholic. I knelt in the pew beside my handsome, ardent husband, bowed my head, when suddenly that new prayer burst up again, from the shadows.

"Dear God, please help me make this marriage work."

*In dinghy: Sarah and Andrew Brady, Bert Wickersham, Sally and
Nathaniel Brady; outside dinghy: Upton, Dot and Frank Ryder,
Peter Wickersham, Joan and Clark Wickersham.
Woods Hole, Massachusetts, 1967.*

PHOTOGRAPH BY DOROTHY I. CROSSLEY

4

There is so much good and evil in
breaking secrets . . .

—G. K. CHESTERTON

In the past nineteen days I have seen my husband die, been surrounded by children and grandchildren, celebrated Easter,
driven two hundred miles and back to scatter Upton's ashes and
another two hundred miles and back for his memorial service. I
am drained. Andrew and his family left four days ago, and I am
trying to get used to every day in this house without Upton in it.
I wake up at night, puzzled by the quiet room—no stertorous
breathing, no warm friend beside me. During the day, I find myself listening for him, waiting to hear his cough; his feet on the
stairs; his soft admonitions to Marilyn, the cat; his deep, weary
sigh. I look at the parade of pills marching across his bureau, so
many pills for so many problems: depression (three different prescriptions), heart disease (two), high cholesterol, high blood pressure, indigestion, insomnia.

This reminds me that I have an appointment with our doctor

tomorrow. When I had my checkup last fall, she urged me to lose fifteen pounds, which I've done, and to keep an eye on my blood pressure. Upton took his blood pressure every morning, and sometimes he took mine, too. I decide to do this myself and take the cuff from the top drawer of his bedside table, where it lies beneath a yellow legal pad. Here, Upton kept a meticulous daily record of his blood pressure and pulse and the temperature outside and sometimes made a note about the weather: *Icy!* or *Sun!* I look at the last entry, written the morning of the day he died. His pulse and blood pressure were within his ideal range, and he'd written *Snow!* in the margin. Once again, my breath catches when I see his handwriting.

When I start to put on the blood pressure cuff, I realize that I don't exactly know what I'm doing, and I look in the drawer for the instructions. I find Kleenex, a pencil, a lifelike plastic cockroach that appeared in Upton's Christmas stocking years ago, matches with the old Atlantic Monthly logo and a jar of Albolene lubricant. The Albolene makes me think of how long it had been since our years of good sex, which ended when Upton became clinically depressed fifteen years ago. I open the jar of Albolene; the ointment is still soft and fresh-looking. What had happened to our intimate lives?

The sphygmomanometer directions aren't in his top drawer, so I open the next one. There's a stethoscope, and beneath it, our friend Chris Tilghman's collection of short stories, *The Way People Run,* something I'd meant to read when it first came out three years ago. I pick it up only to find that the dust jacket doesn't hold a sturdy book, it holds something flimsy. One, two, three, slim, slippery magazines. Beautiful, nude young men with gleaming bodies and gigantic erections smile invitingly at me as I sit on Upton's side of the bed, the blood pressure cuff dangling from my arm. I take several deep breaths, feeling suddenly oxygen-deprived and slightly sick. I carefully slip the naked men into Chris's dust jacket again and shut them back in the drawer, the stethoscope on top. I keep on breathing. I want to wash my hands.

Now what? My bedroom has been invaded. Strangers have been in here, and Upton is one of them, never mind the familiar clothes that still hold his scent hanging in the open closet, or the slippers still waiting by his side of the bed. I feel as though there has been violence in this room, in this bed, though I can't lucidly explain it. I feel deceived, abandoned, and vulnerable. I feel violated. I want to call the children, tell them, defuse this. But what good will that do? And more important, what harm?

I open the drawer and take the porn back out. I can't look at the men on the cover. If I had a knife, I might slash their perfect, beckoning faces. I flip through some pages. The pictures inside are more disturbing. It finally dawns on me that their purpose was to turn my husband on, something I thought was my exclusive privilege. The only magazine I've seen remotely like this was a copy of *Playgirl* years ago, with a story by a writer I knew. I remember thinking at the time that *Playgirl* was trashy. But it didn't repulse me or threaten me the way these three do now.

I see there are stories here, too, and start to read one. The first two sentences are so badly written I can't imagine Upton ever actually reading this. I want to throw them all out, but like a detective or a lawyer collecting evidence, I put them back in the drawer.

I surrender to a flood of sorrow—first the self-pitying sorrow of a spurned lover; then sorrow for the sex we'd only rarely shared the last fifteen years; and finally sorrow for Upton and the great burden of his secret. How could I have not known he was gay? Or did I know? What did I know? What did I know that I didn't know I knew until this minute?

BEDFORD, MASSACHUSETTS, JANUARY 1970

It was after ten on Friday night and Upton still wasn't home. He'd called at six to say he was having drinks with our old friend Edward.

"I'll be home as soon as I can extricate myself."

Upton had gone from lowly college traveler at Knopf to associate editor at McGraw-Hill, and then in 1965, he became managing editor of the Atlantic Monthly Press, an imprint of Little, Brown in Boston. We moved to Cambridge, with Sarah, then two, and Andrew, almost one. In May 1967, after months of religious instruction, I joined the Catholic Church, and a few weeks later, on my twenty-eighth birthday, I gave birth to Nathaniel. The following spring, with Alexander on the way, we moved again, this time to a large family compound in Bedford, twenty miles to the west. The family had been friends of my parents' for many years; some of them had lived with us for brief periods, and one of the daughters was a bridesmaid in my sister's wedding. We rented an old, rambling farmhouse on five hundred acres of undeveloped land with views to the Concord River, with use of a swimming pool and a tennis court that we shared with five other households.

Somewhere in those busy years, Edward turned up, having taken a new job as a marketing consultant in Boston. Upton, always abrasive to Edward when they sparred intellectually, as they'd done from the start, called him Egregious Edward or Edweird behind his back. Edward came out to Sunday lunch quite often. He seemed to delight in the children and our boisterous family life and didn't mind Upton's not always treating him kindly. I told Upton I thought we should invite Edward for Christmas dinner.

"Why?" Upton wrinkled his nose.

"He just moved—he might be lonely." Wasn't this obvious?

"Well," said Upton, "if you must."

Edward came with many presents, including a long, expandable tunnel for the children, which he was very proud of, and which the children loved. Upton hadn't been very nice to Edward on Christmas, not appreciative of the tunnel, or of the wine he'd brought. That was less than a month ago.

I looked at my watch again, and out at the snow-covered fields and the empty road. Upton was drinking more than ever these days, and the drive from Boston to Bedford was long, especially in the chilly little Citroën deux chevaux. I hoped he'd at least had something to eat. There had been many nights during the seven years of our marriage when I'd worried about him getting home safely, imagining him dead on the highway or injured in a hospital. The year we moved to Coney Island (no longer able to afford to stay on Manhattan's fashionable Upper East Side), there were a few nights when I wondered if he'd been attacked by gangs on the subway or on the dangerous Coney Island streets. One night he didn't call or come home at all until morning. He said he'd fallen asleep (passed out, I believe would be more accurate) on the subway, and had ridden back and forth between Coney Island and the Bronx all night. I was never convinced that that had really happened, but all that mattered was that he'd gotten safely home.

But where was Upton now, tonight? I wrapped up what should have been his dinner and put it in the refrigerator, turned out all the lights but one, and went up to bed, trying not to imagine the worst as I checked on each of the four children, so beautiful, so safe in their beds. At eleven-fifteen, Upton called, very drunk, from Edward's, where he said he was spending the night. Thank God. He slurred his words, and his voice was pitiful, apologetic, like a child's. I could hear Edward laughing in the background, and the clink of glasses when Upton paused to inhale his cigarette. I wished he were asleep beside me, breathing peacefully like his children. But at least he was safe.

Alone in our bed, I didn't fall asleep even though I was exhausted. I thought about how our lives had changed when Upton joined the venerable Atlantic Monthly Press and we were swept into the dazzle of mainstream publishing. There were dinners with Pauline Kael at the Ritz, elegant parties at Edward Weeks's house on Beacon Hill for Peter Ustinov and Agnes de Mille, Sunday lunches here in Bedford with Faye Dunaway, Jose Luis Sert, and William Least Heat Moon. Upton and I put on intimate dinners for eight and book parties for eighty. We knew how to make parties work, what people to put together, and how to make them feel at ease. The food was good and abundant, and everyone's glass was full.

But when it was just the two of us, the slightest difference of opinion could trigger a burst of rage, a lecture, a stream of burning criticism directed at me. Upton's tantrums were similar to my mother's and familiar territory except that I automatically accepted the blame for Upton's outbursts, often believing that something I had mistakenly done or not done was the cause. Lately, however, I'd begun to wonder. Upton's accusations didn't always make sense. He blamed me for things I hadn't done, for thoughts I never had. Sometimes it was as if someone else had taken my place, a monster Sally, whom I didn't know and couldn't banish.

Tomorrow was Saturday. I would get up early and clean the house, have things in order when Upton got home. He'd probably be a bit hungover, and maybe an orderly house would make him feel better. I fell asleep thinking of things I should try to do before he got back—wash kitchen floor, empty trash, change kitty litter, polish candlesticks . . .

When Upton drove in, looking rumpled and hungover, the house was clean and I was giving the children lunch. He poured himself some coffee and went upstairs to shower and change his clothes. By the time he came back down, the children were fed and in their rooms for naps. We had the house to ourselves for the next two hours. Upton made himself a martini, and I made us each the Saturday grilled cheese sandwich.

"Sally—" Upton rarely called me by my name. He would do it when he was very angry, or upset, or when he hollered at me from a distance.

I looked at him, slumped over his sandwich. He looked broken.

"I need to talk to you."

I put my hand on the back of his neck, and he looked up, shaking off my hand. His eyes were still bloodshot, the whites thick and almost yellow, the blue dull. His skin looked grayish and damp, not tight and rosy the way it usually did.

"Are you all right?" Now I put my hand on his forehead, briefly, as if he were one of the children. No fever.

He didn't meet my eyes. I waited while he took a breath.

"I had sex with Edward."

Even now, forty years later, as I write the words I am still stunned, still overwhelmed by the shock of this truth. At the time, I was frozen, unable to speak, or even to think. I had imagined Upton dead, beaten up, in jail for DWI. I had imagined him so angry he would strike me. But I had never imagined Upton having sex with another man, and certainly not with Edward. In fact, I'd never imagined Upton having sex with anyone except me.

"I'm sorry," he said, his voice breaking.

He paused, maybe waiting for me to say something but I couldn't. I had no words at all.

"It was because I was drunk."

I waited for him to go on.

"It had nothing to do with you."

The silence in the kitchen crackled.

Finally I said something. "Was this the first time?"

Another pause. "No."

"How many times has it happened?" This seemed terribly important to me, though I knew I wasn't thinking clearly.

Upton, eyes on his martini glass, raised his shoulders as if he didn't know. Then in a flash he picked up his glass, knocked back the rest of the martini, and pushed away his untouched sandwich. I knew that was it. Upton had shut down; the subject was closed.

"What are we going to do?"

Again the shrug.

Suddenly I was afraid. Our lives were changing right now, in this very minute. This was a turning point, and I was in it, trying to stop the spinning. Did he want to move in with Edward? They were lovers, after all. I forced this thought on myself. But Upton and I were lovers, too. Was I to give him up?

We would have to make some sort of an arrangement. I didn't know yet what it would be, but we would find a way for Upton to love Edward if that is what he had to do, and still be part of this family. I didn't want Edward to be part of this family, certainly not. But I didn't want to lose Upton. If he preferred men, how could I expect or want him to stay married to me? If he didn't want to make love to me, I didn't want him to have to. None of this meant I would accept a celibate life; that hardly would be fair. There were so many things to consider, and now they were rushing at me, rushing past me, in a blizzard.

"Upton, what are we going to do?"

"What do you mean?"

Was this a challenge or did he really want to know what I was thinking? I watched him pour the rest of the martini into his empty glass, hold it to the light, and take a big swig. I waited while his tongue swept his lips. He put down the glass and looked at me.

"I told you it had nothing to do with you. I said it only happened because I was drunk." He was sounding defensive now, almost angry.

"But it does have something to do with me." And I needed more information; I wanted stepping-stones of concrete facts to show me the way out. I needed to know if Upton wanted to leave me, and if he would have sex with Edward again. I thought about how it could have happened not just once but several times before. When? Where? Not our bed, please not there. When was the first time? The second? We'd known Edward before we were married—had they had sex together then? Was Upton mean to Edward because Edward had seduced him? Had Upton had sex with other men? Other men—this stopped me cold. Did he realize or even believe that he had broken his sacred vows of matrimony: "*. . . keeping yourself only unto her as long as you both shall live?*"

"What are we going to do?" I asked him again. So many questions, yet I was stuck on this particular one. Was it because of all my questions, this was probably the only one that would eventually be answered?

"Do?" Upton slammed his glass on the table. "Well, you could pay a little more attention to me, for one thing."

I was not prepared for this. His words stung.

Had I not been attentive? It seemed to me that Upton had always been the focus of the household. The children, even the toddlers, knew to pick up their toys before Pa came home; to be quiet during "grown-up time," a euphemism for cocktails. Sarah was only six and she knew which fork to set at his place at the table. Every night I worried that I might not have the children in bed and Upton's and my dinner on the table by 7:30. According to Upton, dinner at 7:33 was the same as dinner at 7:45. Late was late; minutes didn't matter. I began to feel the familiar finger of guilt worming its way in. And fear, too, that he would fly into a fury.

"If you were more available"—Upton's voice took on an accusatory pitch—"I wouldn't have to go somewhere else for sex."

Available? Yes, four children in five years did cut back on availability. But not as often as alcohol. When Upton drank too much, liquor first made him amorous and then left him impotent. He would announce this in a British accent, like Michael Flanders: "The evil gin does is hard to assess, and besides, it's inclined to affect me prowess. So have some Madeira, m'dear," and I was expected to laugh. I couldn't figure out why impotence didn't upset him, but I did figure out that the most reliable times for sex with Upton were before we got up in the morning, before lunch, or after his nap. Besides, I didn't want a slobbering lover who slurred his words and couldn't focus his bloodshot eyes. But I didn't point this out, veering away from his anger to my own guilt, or was it shame? My neglect had driven him to the bed of another man. It was my fault. For having dinner late, being pregnant, tired, full of milk, not available. I burst into tears, and ran up to our bedroom.

Upton followed, took me in his arms. "Sally, Sally." His voice was raspy and defeated. "I give you my promise, it will never happen again. Never. I give you my word." I stayed in his arms, wanting to believe him, wanting to believe that it wasn't my fault, listening to his heart pound. The next day, Sunday, I told Upton that I needed to get away and think about things, and that he would have to take care of the children. I threw my skis in the back of the car—exercise can often help—and drove north, letting the fragmented thoughts from the day before cut in and out like the broken white lines on the road.

Was Upton truly homosexual or were the incidents with Edward drunken seductions? Upton's multifaceted talents—he didn't only sew, he knew how to hand-smock dresses for Sarah, he designed and embroidered monograms; he didn't just cook, he made roses from icing and from radishes, too. He knew how to figure-skate and was an accomplished diver. He danced. And I loved him for all these unmanly passions and accomplishments, many of which he taught me to do. I had never cooked, cleaned, or sewn a hem until I was twenty-one. I didn't even learn to drive a car until Natty was born.

The first winter we were married I was asked to help with the re-creation of the 1912 Armory Art Show, a notable New York society event as well as a milestone in the art world. The Gala Opening was in May 1963, a month before Sarah was born, a black-tie evening with dinner parties beforehand and dancing parties afterward. Upton's and my closet was full of fancy clothes—the General's tailcoat, morning coat, and dinner jacket along with accompanying accoutrements on Upton's side, and floor-length silks and velvets on mine, with a row of treacherous little evening slippers on the floor below.

But eight months pregnant, I had nothing to wear to the Gala Opening. We may have been charming and known how to grace a party, but we were living on twelve dollars a week, for food and incidentals. There was nothing in the budget for clothes. Upton had made most of my maternity clothes from fabric we had on hand. But the supply was exhausted. Except for one beautiful bolt of white sari silk shot through with gold. I took it down from its hiding place in the back of the closet, still wrapped in blue tissue paper.

"Where did this come from?" Upton eyed the yards and yards of filmy white silk and gold, knowing I couldn't have bought it.

"Liberty," I said.

"London?"

I nodded. He waited for me to say more. "Nikos brought it to me a long time ago." It wasn't that long ago, not even two years, but in that moment, it seemed a lifetime.

A week later, I swept into the 69th Regiment Armory in a gold-and-white Empire gown, strapless, "to accentuate the positive," said Upton, meaning my new milky bosom. He encased sturdy two-inch-wide elastic in a strip of gold sari border and ran it under my breasts and above the baby bulge in front, and then made it disappear, to circle my back beneath the folds of cascading white parachute silk. It was a brilliant construction and made me look and feel like a graceful, fertile beauty. According to *Women's Wear Daily*, the precursor to *W,* there were three saris at the opening: a Mainbocher, a Givenchy, and an Upton. Did this make him a homosexual? This was a brand-new and frightening thought to me.

If Upton wanted to be free to love men, could we keep on living together in the same house? If the only solution was to separate, and have two different households, how would we manage when there was barely enough money for one household? I had no real skills, no college degree, no trust fund. We had four very young children, and one old car that needed work. We didn't own our house. My parents couldn't give me much financial help, and the children and I certainly couldn't live with them. Those were the minuses.

The pluses? I was healthy, smart, and energetic. I could cook and clean and garden. I knew many rich people with big houses. Good help was hard to get. I could probably find someone with an empty servants' wing who needed someone like me to run their house. A rich person with a big house who didn't mind four young children. It might even be an interesting change. In time, I might fall in love with someone else and have a whole new life. Not much of a plan, but it was all I could come up with right then.

That Upton had deceived me with a man made me feel helpless. An affair with another woman might just be a passing dalliance. But if Upton preferred men, why would he choose to stay with me for the rest of his life? How could he think that whatever he did with Edward had nothing to do with me? How could he possibly think that sex with anyone else did not have something to do with me? I was his wife. We had vowed to be partners for life. To consciously exclude me, of itself, meant I was involved, didn't it? And to want to exclude me, to think it was even possible to exclude me when it came to sex, was almost as if his contempt for Edward was precisely because Edward was homosexual. Could you be a homophobic homosexual?

I thought of Gray, a respected New York editor whose company we both enjoyed and who I assumed was homosexual though Upton and I had never mentioned it. Occasionally, he and Upton would meet after work for drinks. On one such night, Upton, tight, called to tell me he was staying at Gray's— it was too late and he was too tired to come home. I was glad he would be safe. The night he'd said he'd fallen asleep on the subway he had also been with Gray. I was shocked at myself for even considering that this dignified friend of both of ours might have seduced Upton. The mere suspicion now, years later, made me feel guilty for thinking it.

I went back in my mind even further, to the year with Lib in New York and a party at the apartment. Upton and Buff were there, and a stuffed shirt named Piers, whom neither Lib nor I liked particularly. He came with a robust trust fund, a well-bred lisp, and a striking Dutch woman, known for removing her clothes at parties. She was really the reason we'd invited him, and she turned out to be a big disappointment—the only thing she took off was her coat. I wasn't happy when late in the evening Piers cornered me in the hall, and with a disgusted curl to his thin upper lip asked me what I was doing with those two "queerth," pointing to Upton and Buff.

I was furious. This was a devastating and false accusation, as damaging as calling someone a liar or a thief, and unthought-of to announce in public.

"You don't know what you're talking about." I spat out the words.

"Oh, yeth I do." He grinned. "Queer ath three-dollar billth. Both of them."

I stared at the lisper's narrow face, at his mean mouth and the tilt of his weak chin. I looked him in the eye and said very clearly, "That'th ridiculouth."

I realized that I'd replayed that scene several times in the busy nine years since it had taken place. What I should have said, of course, is "How do *you* know?" But at the time, it didn't cross my mind. Or did it, and I just didn't want to know the answer?

Buff and Lib had remained engaged for well over a year, with Lib in London and Buff in Cambridge. There were never any concrete marriage plans, nor was the engagement ever called off. In late spring 1965, Buff married Mary, half Irish, half Lebanese, and beautiful as a ripe plum. Their son was born seven months later. Upton was Buff's best man, as Buff had been Upton's. And soon after that, Lib, still in London, married Bruce Chatwin. Upton, for no reason that I was aware of, became testy about Buff. There had always been a good-natured rivalry among all three Brady men: Buff was the athlete, Jem was the scholar, and Upton was a little of both. But after Buff got married, Upton became unreasonably critical of him, and I had no idea why. Of course, Upton wouldn't discuss it, but Buff was living in New York and we were in Bedford, so except for big family parties, we didn't see him often, which was probably just as well.

Crossing into New Hampshire, I tried to imagine leaving Upton and living a life without him. I couldn't. Even with his drinking, he was such a vital component to each of my days. I loved what he had to say and how he savored saying it, in Greek or Latin or Shakespearean verse; I loved seeing the world through his remarkable lens of knowledge. Whatever Upton did, and there seemed to be no limit to his skills, he did with such fervor and pleasure that I wanted to do it, too. I loved the way he made love to me—he was a generous and attentive lover when he wasn't drunk. I loved watching him get dressed; his well-proportioned body, which fit mine so perfectly, was beautiful to watch from naked to boxer shorts to silky Brooks Brothers shirt to three-piece suit and Liberty tie. Garters held up his dark socks—no glimpse of white ankle when Upton crossed his legs. His shoes were always shined.

I loved the way we filled the pew in church on Sunday, everyone ironed and brushed, praying together, singing the hymns all the way home in the car. Just recently we'd discovered that the sappy words to a new and over-sung hymn could be replaced with any Shakespearean sonnet. Sunday after Sunday we substituted "Shall I compare thee to a summer's day" or "When to the sessions of sweet silent thought" for "Oh Lord, at thy first Eucharistic Feast," singing lustily between hiccups of laughter. Upton was openly amazed by and in love with his children. He laughed with them when sometimes I didn't, taught them things I didn't know—how to tie complicated knots and turn them into lanyards, for instance, or how to transform a plain old damask napkin into a puppet while you were waiting for dessert. We beat each other at Scrabble, fought over the *New York Times* crossword puzzle, played duets on our recorders, read aloud to each other in bed. And there was the dancing, always the dancing—the two of us in the kitchen, or in Boston at the Viennese Evenings, whirling across the slippery floor in all our finery. I couldn't lose all this.

Whatever had happened with Edward was over. Upton had given me his word, and I would believe him. At the same time, I believed that in some crucial way that I didn't understand, I had let Upton down. Driving north, getting into the mountains, I kept circling back to this. What had happened with Edward was partly my fault. There was no doubt in my mind. If I had acted differently, if I had done something else, been more attentive, for instance, Upton would not have been tempted to go off with another man. Or would he? Was it my fault? Partly my fault? Was I the only one who could keep Upton from wanting sex with Edward? To keep Upton from being "queer ath a three-dollar bill"?

And then, with those words, I suddenly understood Upton's desperation to marry me. He was sure that if he married me, a desirable young woman who desired him, and if he fathered children, he would be cured. Marriage to me would change everything. He would not be a fairy, a homo; he would not be "queer ath a three-dollar bill." This is why Upton had been so determined to marry me, and so desperate when he thought I might not go through with the wedding. This was why he thought he could not live without me. This was the true heartbreak.

I had been driving for hours, letting all these thoughts swim in and out. But now, somewhere in mountainous New Hampshire, I understood how Upton's magic had failed him. He must be very scared and very sad. I turned the car around and headed back, skis untouched in the trunk. I pulled into the dark driveway. The children were in their pajamas, clean, fed, and ready for bed, clumped around Upton in the living room while he read to them in front of the fire. He was not drunk. Dinner was in the oven. We would put all this behind us.

Upton was what he was. He was Upton, my handsome, gifted, troubled husband. He would keep his word. We would not talk of this again, I was sure. We would move on. Upton had said he couldn't live without me. But the real heart of this was that in spite of everything, I didn't want to live without him. We belonged together, I was sure of it.

VERMONT, STILL APRIL 2008

Day and night, I catch myself stumbling on regrets—did Upton know how much I loved it when we held hands every morning and checked in to see how we were feeling, and talked about what was on our minds? Twenty years ago, he proposed that every day we have this early moment together, before the business of living swept us away. I would turn off the phone, shut the door on children or guests, no interruptions for fifteen minutes. It was initially supposed to be a time when we could talk openly, air any grievances or worries. But for the past few years, we had let the grievances go and would sit at the table, holding hands, connecting with each other.

"How are you?" we would ask.

"What would you like for dinner?"

"Look! The goldfinches are beginning to turn yellow."

"Thank you for folding my laundry."

Little things. Little things that I now see were really the big things. I think this is something Upton understood all along. But I was waiting for something bigger, more dramatic, a huge epiphany when the curtain went up and Upton declared his passion for me, said how in spite of everything, he felt blessed to be married to me. He would take me in his arms, tell me how he loved my humor, my generosity, my mind, my body, my spirit. The violins would swell. Every day, while he held my hand, a part of me was waiting for the big production, unaware that it was taking place right there on the table next to the unfinished coffee and the daily horoscope from the *Valley News*.

I think about the dolphin I saw in Florida a year ago. Joan and I were staying in a motel on Vanderbilt Beach in North

Naples, as we have every spring for the past ten years. It was our first day, and I began it as always, with a walk on the beach outside our screened porch, eager to see egrets, willets, pelicans, and other wonders, especially hoping there would be dolphins cavorting in the calm, early-morning sea. And there was one, just one, a single dolphin very close to shore. Dolphins usually swim in couples or in pods, rarely alone. And usually they don't swim in the shallows. I stopped to watch. He was close to the surface and swam in frantic, tight circles. There was nothing playful about this dolphin. I was caught by his frenzy.

The next morning, I saw him again, in the same shallow water, still swimming in circles. The third morning another person stopped to watch, a marine biologist.

"He's lost his mate," she said. "They do this for six weeks or so, marking the spot they were last together. Dolphins mate for life."

Every day for a week, I watched the dolphin. On the last morning, he wasn't there. I imagined him as the sun rose, finished at last with circling, swimming out alone into the wide, deep sea.

No wonder I'd believed for all these years that sex with Edward was only a drunken dalliance. I can't stop crying, and I can't sort out my feelings. Betrayal is surely one, and sorrow for Upton's shameful secret life, and anger that he isn't here to tell me what really happened. This makes me laugh, even though I'm crying, because if Upton were alive, it wouldn't make any difference—I still wouldn't know if he'd kept his long-ago promise, or if he'd given in to other lovers, or if the gay porn was his way of keeping that promise. Upton would not have told me. He would have shut down and not said a single word. I am sure of that. The darkness of not knowing is pulling me down. I decide to call the children.

First Alex. He's a ballet dancer—straight, but so familiar with this new world we live in, where we can be openly gay or straight or bi. It is easy for me to talk with him about almost anything. I tell him I have found gay porn, and then I tell him about Upton's encounters with Edward. I don't say that Edward was a predator who took advantage of Upton and seduced him when he was drunk, even though that's what I believe. I just say they had sex. More than once. And that Upton had given me his word it would never happen again.

"Wow." Alex takes a deep breath. "I just felt a click. I mean, I always knew Pa loved me, that was clear, but there was something—a curtain—that kept him apart. And this is what it was."

Sarah is next, and sympathetic, with more than just a glimmer of how this all must be for me. Natty, too, is very kind to me, but stunned. I think this news hits him the hardest.

Finally, I call Andrew. I'd saved him for last, wanting to have three run-throughs first. Andrew is smart. He can cut right to the quick. I have no idea what he will say, or how I might react to his reaction. There is only the briefest pause after I give him the news.

And then, in a very loud voice, he says, "Mom, get over it! It's only porn!"

I murmur something about betrayal and Andrew rolls in again, drowning me out.

"Just get over it!" I hear him sigh, know he is impatient. "Remember the prayer I read at Pa's service? 'What has been done has been done; let it be.'"

I don't answer; those lines have been running through my head ever since I opened the drawer.

"Mom?"

"Yes, Andrew. I remember."

"Okay, well, that's it."

What I keep from this conversation is "Get over it." Will I? Yes, probably. But not yet. There is so much I don't know, and so much I probably do know, and I will keep exploring, going back and further back, again and again, looking for clues, for the truth. There have been enough secrets; I want to throw open the windows, let in the light.

What has been done has certainly been done. But how can I *let it be*? I have been living a lie for forty-six years, and I need to find the truth.

No, I don't have it quite right. It was Upton who actually *lived* the lie. I only lived *with* the lie. And loved the liar. I think of all the years of my "Help me make this marriage work" prayer. And of how Upton always used to say, with a chuckle, "It's the answered prayers you have to worry about."

Andrew, Sally, Alex, Sarah, Natty.
Bedford, Massachusetts, 1970.

PHOTOGRAPH BY DAVID BIDDLE

5

How lonely and unnatural man is and how deep
and well-concealed are his confusions.

—JOHN CHEEVER

VERMONT, APRIL 17, 2008

Today is Upton's seventieth birthday. Sarah and her two boys,
Max and Zachary, are coming this afternoon, and even though
it's only been a week since Andrew, Mari, and their young ones
left, only a week since I found the porn, I am very glad to have
this new wave of children to distract me. Sarah wondered if
we should have a cake to celebrate the birthday, but I said no. It
seems wrong to me, to celebrate Upton's birth right now when I
am still stumbling through his death. I wonder briefly if a celebration would be good for the boys, but no, I think it might be
confusing.

Winter finally is turning its back. I can feel the hard, frozen
ground letting go, water rushing downhill everywhere. In the
cellar, the sump pump has sprung to life, while aboveground,
cataracts tumble through the porous snow on every slope and the
dirt road is slick and soft where the sun has thawed the surface.

Yesterday I saw a redwing blackbird, and maybe tonight we'll hear the first chirp of the spring peepers from the pond. I go over these old signs of spring to get used to the fact that another season is almost here, even though Upton is not.

I'm trying to at least start clearing out some of his things, because I think I'm supposed to. Yesterday I found out I can't give away any of his expensive prescription meds, not even the unopened ones, and now I put them all in a shoe box marked HAZARDOUS WASTE to go to the dump. I pause. For now, this is as far as I can go clearing off his bureau. I don't want to do it; it seems too soon. And besides, I like having his personal stuff right here, where it's always been—his comb next to the small pottery pitcher he brought back from Spain in 1957 when he was still at Harvard. The pitcher holds pencils, pens, a nail file, and a tiny screwdriver for fixing eyeglasses, very useful.

I think about going through his bureau drawers, pull one open and bring a folded T-shirt to my nose. I still can smell him in so many places, and wonder what it will be like when eventually that, too, is gone. I put the T-shirt back and shut the drawer. That's it for drawers, I'm still gun-shy, not up for more surprises. Tomorrow I go to the probate court with Upton's will, death certificate, and last bank statement, the bill from the undertaker, and the list of creditors that Sarah compiled. I'm dreading it and glad Sarah and the boys will be here to bolster my spirits. The phone rings night and day, creditors calling to harass me. I am falling in love with caller ID.

I scan the bedroom for anything else I can take to the dump with the meds. Something I won't have to open or go through. The nook under the eaves where we keep our luggage is an over-flowing mess. Half the suitcases haven't been used in years and are thick with dust. I'll get rid of them, clean out something, at least. I heave a heavy pre-wheeled bag of mine into the middle of the room and then haul out one of Upton's, the canvas stiff with age, its compartments unzipped and unwieldy. I throw it on top of mine and something comes clattering out. A video box. I pick it up. A threesome of naked men having fun on the cover. Upton, Upton. My stomach lurches, and I can feel the acid from my coffee rising. I shake the suitcase hard and more videos tumble out, six in all.

I put them in a plastic bag, tie it up, and put it next to the hazardous waste box. I think of putting the meds in the bag and labeling it all HAZARDOUS WASTE. Isn't that what it is? Will this never end? I'm furious and in tears. What if eight-year-old Max had found the videos? Or opened the drawer with the magazines? What else am I going to discover? Oh, Upton, how could you do this? You, who were always so meticulous, so careful?

I can't sort out the pieces that rush at me, and I call my very good friend Trish. Her two sons grew up with Natty and Alex in Bedford, and Trish was a loyal confidante through the hardest years of my marriage, when I wondered if I could stick it out. I tell her about the magazines and the videos. She doesn't say anything for a long minute. Then she tells me this:

"I vowed I would take this to my grave," she begins. "Remember the summer Eric worked at the Lexington Pharmacy, 1988 or '89?" And she tells me about the day when he was at the checkout and Upton approached with an armful of gay porn. Eric had been Alex's best friend growing up, but Upton didn't expect to see him at the cash register in the Lexington drugstore, and he didn't recognize him until it was too late to turn back. Eric rang up the sale, Upton left, and Eric, shaken, told his mother about it as soon as he got home. It would have been so easy for Trish to have told me years ago, or for Eric to have told Alex, except that Eric wouldn't have; he's not that kind of friend. This must have felt like a close call to Upton.

On the floor of his closet I see the navy blue Atlantic Monthly bag he used when we went to the beach. This brings back good memories of peaceful Sundays at Plum Island with the children, picnics under the "pavilion," the children's word for the canopy Upton would rig with a sheet, string, and four driftwood posts. We feasted on freshly gathered mussels steaming over the driftwood fire in the sand pit, took long walks at low tide on the hard sand, napped. When we were alone, which was rare, one of us would wake the other with a wandering hand and we would make discreet love beneath a damp towel.

Upton always kept his beach bag neatly packed and ready so he could take off at a sunny minute's notice on a hot day. I open it now, pretty sure I won't find any horrible surprises in here. There is his small, silky bathing suit. He used to call it his fig leaf. Our friend Hoima used to call it a *cache-misère*. I go through the rest of the bag: one carefully folded clean beach towel, a small bottle of shampoo, a comb, sunblock, Off!, Lubriderm lotion, and at the bottom, the beloved bathing suit clip.

Upton made this long ago when we were at the Cove. He tied one end of four feet of chalk line to an empty travel-size shampoo bottle that served as a buoy, threaded and knotted the line through several wooden clothespins, and then tied a small, heavy piece of hardware to the other end as an anchor. We had discreetly skinny-dipped everywhere with this, wading out into chest-deep water, taking off our suits and clipping them on to the clothespins. Once, at the Cove when the tide was running, I did a hasty job of clipping and my bikini top drifted off to Martha's Vineyard, which we thought was hilarious.

Just thinking of this and remembering how it feels to float naked in the cool, clear water has calmed me down. I put the bathing suit clip in my own drawer and return Upton's beach bag to the closet. The last time Upton carried it was August, in Woods Hole. Nine months ago. Back in Vermont, Upton had washed his bathing suit and towel and repacked his bag for this summer, which soon will arrive without him.

I pick up my various hazardous wastes. That's enough for this early spring morning. Happy Birthday, Upton. Tomorrow, the probate court. One by one, at least some of the secrets emerge into the light.

BEDFORD, 1971–1974

Upton's anger and drinking moved like Siamese twins through our lives. The shadow of his affair, or whatever it was with Edward, lurked in corners, but most of the time I looked away, knowing Upton was a man of honor and would be true to his word. He said it was over. He said it would never happen again. And he made these promises with such distaste, such loathing of what he had done, that of course I believed him.

In spite of his drinking, Upton was never late for work, never late for anything; he was always impeccably dressed, organized, energetic. He left home a few minutes before the school bus came, gulping only black coffee while I served up scrambled eggs and bacon to everyone else. Upton refused even a slice of toasted homemade bread, or a splash of cream in his coffee.

Every day he arrived at the Atlantic an hour early, and with more black coffee, turned his wonderful mind to the business of publishing books. At twelve-thirty, on a still-empty stomach, he walked to the Ritz bar for a two-martini lunch. After lunch, he might walk back through the Public Garden across the street, sobering up while he took in the formal seasonal plantings of tulips or roses or chrysanthemums. In the winter, he kept a pair of skates in his office for the rare days when there was skating on the Frog Pond. This is when he started to espouse the afternoon nap, just twenty minutes stretched out on the rug in his office. The first time he did it, his secretary came in unexpectedly and thought he was dead. It was the only way he could drink at lunch and still be able to work.

Upton rolled home around six-thirty, hungover from lunch and desperate for his bourbon. I would have a frisson of fear when I heard the deux chevaux splutter to a stop in the driveway. Bikes and soccer balls scattered on the lawn? Big Wheels on the porch? Boots not lined up in tidy ranks in the back hall? An errant red caboose or G.I. Joe abandoned in the living room? Any one of these could tip Upton into a fury. It was like navigating shifting shoals for me and for the children, even though I tried to protect them by feeding them an early supper and letting Upton settle in with his whiskey while I put them to bed or settled them down with homework. How wrong I had been before we got married, thinking Upton shared my dream of a house filled with lively children and a certain unpredictable and creative disorder. What Upton really craved was my undivided attention and compliance, and an unchanging adult routine at home.

When I came downstairs, I'd have a glass of wine, light the candles, and serve up dinner for the two of us. Expansive and charming with just the right amount to drink, Upton would tell me about his day, lively accounts filled with erudite quotes and colorful anecdotes of authors and editors. Or he would complain about his dealings with Peter Davison, the director of the press and someone with whom Upton had many wrenching differences in the almost twenty-five years they worked together.

After dinner and another whiskey, this time with more water, Upton would put some music on the stereo—Mozart or Haydn—take out the Scrabble or backgammon board, and we would play through a haze of cigarette smoke. He loved games. Games had rules; everything was black or white, no gray areas. Conversations, on the other hand, with anyone and especially with me, could be treacherous. They might lead to discussions or worse, negotiations. We might find ourselves in emotional quicksand, with no rules, no safety net, no boundaries. Backgammon and Scrabble boards became our battlegrounds. I didn't know why Upton was so frightened of feelings, only that he was. And I knew that his fear so easily erupted into rage. A certain level of alcohol kept him mellow, in control, and at his dazzling best. But with one swallow too many, this could change in an instant, and I didn't know how to prevent it or end it. Most nights, I would leave him nursing his drink and go up to bed. My days started early and were often exhausting.

I didn't usually notice when Upton slid in beside me, but once in a while I would startle awake, feeling the empty space where he should have been. I worried that he might have passed out in front of the fire, without putting up the screen or putting out his cigarette, and would get up to look for him. I never did find him passed out. But several times I came upon him in the dark hall, leaning in the open doorway of one of the children's rooms, watching his sleeping child. I never let him know I saw him, never mentioned the surge of compassion I felt seeing his moonlit face so full of tenderness and wonder. There was a naked surrender in his vigil, and I think if he had caught me watching him he would have felt violated.

At Sunday lunch we all ate together, the one reliable time when we lived my premarital dream of the sunny children around the food-laden table, the handsome father carving the roast, the pretty mother helping the baby with his bib, a classy Norman Rockwell gathering, only with martinis first and then with wine. Egregious Edward was no longer a frequent visitor but there were many others, for lunch, dinner, parties. When Jem got married, we had a dinner dance the night before and a wedding brunch the day after; there were birthday parties, dances on New Year's Eve, and every year an open house late

Christmas afternoon. I loved giving parties; we were a team—Upton the consummate host and a competent partner before the guests arrived and after they left. He might grumble a bit, but in a fairly good-natured way. I also liked having other people around, not just for their good company but because Upton was much better behaved when we had guests. It was safer for the children and for me when we weren't alone with him.

In March 1971, after a long and difficult winter, Madee died in the Newport hospital, either of liver cancer or cirrhosis or both. Instead of making Buff, the eldest son, executor of her small estate, Madee had designated Upton and Jem as co-executors, which must have been hard for Buff, though I never heard him mention it. The four days of waking and burying Madee was the first time I had been with all five of Upton's brothers and sisters and their spouses for more than a few hours, and it was also the first time we were all together without Madee. Tension hummed in Madee's little house, and the collection of empty Jim Beam bottles grew. But for visiting hours at the funeral home we all put on our best manners, and everyone pitched in to take care of the details of the Resurrection Mass and burial at the Priory, and the reception at Madee's house afterward.

The night before the funeral, we were all on edge. Upton and Buff, both drunk, began to taunt each other, as they often did, but this time they were noisier, drunker, nastier. It was late, and Lucy physically pushed them out of the house into the March night to cool off. I was getting ready for bed when I heard sirens and saw flashing blue lights stop just up the road. Madee's neighbor on the other side of the small field had called 911 when she heard the fighting. A few minutes later, the police drove away and Upton stumbled in, red-faced, rumpled, and scratched. He never told me what the fight was about; all he said when I asked him was "Buff is a liar." He said this more than once, tears streaming down his face, then jumped into a steaming shower and never mentioned it again. If Madee had been alive, the fight never would have happened. She was an emotional lightning rod for her children; she grounded them, gave them the fixed, unbreakable order that held them together, and she instilled in them all a crippling fear that they might not measure up. Bradys were expected to excel, to get it right, for God and family. They certainly didn't have fights that made the neighbors call the police.

After the Mass and burial, Upton and I walked down from the Priory to the shore of Narragansett Bay, he in his white shirt and raw silk tie, dark suit and vest, his polished black shoes incongruous on the shale-strewn shore. The March wind off the water was cold and damp, the sky gray. He let me hold him while he wept, huge shuddering sobs from a sorrow so deep it frightened me. Or maybe what frightened me was seeing how vulnerable Upton was, buffeted in a wild and unpredictable emotional sea of loss and abandonment. Where was the Renaissance man who could do anything? The lover who couldn't live without me? The dancer, the believer in the one, true Church? Upton was all of these things: weak, strong; gay, straight; confident, terrified; brilliant, dim; faithful, unfaithful. Here, on the stony beach, I held all these disparate elements of Upton in my arms. This is the man I married.

In the months after Madee died, Upton was morbidly aware that he was now on the top rung, and he frequently reminded us of this. Only thirty-three, clear-eyed, fair-skinned, and fit, Upton looked more like twenty-three despite the cigarettes and booze. He claimed to hate it when authors meeting him for the first time would say, "Oh, but you're so *young*!" However, without Madee at the helm, Upton seemed marooned in a swirl of whiskey and gin. As executors of their mother's modest estate, he and Jem spent many weekends in Portsmouth over the next several months, going through her files, sorting out the house, and drinking far too much. In spite of all the liquor, they did a meticulous, amazing job of dividing up the spoils among all six children so that everyone more or less got what they wanted and no one felt cheated.

The salaries at the Atlantic were barely enough to live on, and assumed one had some additional income—usually a trust fund—so Upton's $10,000 inheritance was a godsend and just enough to keep us out of debt for a few years. It could also have been a down payment on a house. My parents urged us to think about buying a "starter" house, getting a mortgage and building equity, all terms Upton scorned.

"We can't afford a mortgage for anything I'd want to live in, not with four children!"

When he made such pronouncements, there was no point in responding. His mind was made up. No house. I didn't want to hear him say "*my* money" or, this time, "*my* inheritance." I didn't want to have to dodge his anger, which I always felt was directed at me even though I'm not sure it always was. And I didn't want to hear the sad humiliation behind the anger. I knew Upton felt guilty and ashamed that like his own father, he wasn't earning enough money (or maybe not managing what he did earn wisely enough) to buy a house and support us all in the way he thought he should. Most of the Bradys were haunted by the story of their father's brother, Leo. Handsome as Buff, smart as

Upton, Uncle Leo had died in a shelter in Boston, alcoholic, penniless, broken. Even I had heard the story again and again from Madee, and it always sounded like a warning: *Watch out! This could happen to you, too.*

In February 1972, still flush with his inheritance, Upton invited me to come with him to Los Angeles for the publication of L.A. cop and bestselling author Joseph Wambaugh's second book, *The Blue Knight*, which was dedicated to Upton. Joe and his wife, Dee, had celebrated his literary debut and the publication of *The New Centurions* with us in 1970 with New England revelry at the Ritz in Boston. Now, in 1972, *The New Centurions* was being made into a movie starring Stacy Keach and Joe had become a celebrity. The trip to L.A. would be quite an event. And a few days later, Madame Cecilia Chiang, well known in San Francisco for her elegant Chinese restaurant, Mandarin, was celebrating the publication of her book, part memoir, part recipes.

"I've made reservations at the Beverly Wilshire on Rodeo Drive in L.A.," Upton said, eyes dancing. "Very posh. And at the Maurice in San Francisco, very staid. Here," he said, flourishing a blank check, "go on a shopping spree!"

We had been married almost ten years, our four children shone, our lives were full of interesting people and a certain amount of glamour, but I longed for the easy intimacy Upton and I used to share. I'd expected it would deepen over time and always be a central pulse of our marriage. Sometimes it was there in flashes—on the beach after Madee's funeral, or when we made each other laugh, or had the same intense reaction to an idea, a person, a snippet of song. There was, I believed, a wordless closeness when we made love, and with the birth of each child, and every Sunday in church. But what I yearned for were the times when Upton would reach for my hand for no reason, or pull me close when we looked at the stars on a moonless night. I lived for the small, spontaneous sparks when we could light up each other's lives for just a moment.

What had kept me rooted and whole in my marriage were the children. No longer toddlers who could be sent off to bed, they had become curious, kind creatures, grown wise in the ways of anger and drink, and wise, too, in the complexities and depth of Upton's love. I tried to make it clear that Upton's anger, though sometimes directed at them, was misdirected. I told them over and over again that it was not their fault or my fault that Upton was drinking. Mercifully, the children remained accessible and present. I hugged and kissed and laughed and cried with them from the early days of their warm toddler heads beneath my cheek to their new, ungainly, hard and generous arms circling me in hasty preadolescent hugs. The children and I breathed the same air, while Upton inched away.

It was time for a vacation, just the two of us, alone. Upton flew out a few days ahead of me, stopping in Chicago and Iowa to meet with authors. He managed to make it out of Iowa in the wake of a severe blizzard, but I was in the thick of it, my plane several hours delayed before it even left Boston. By the time we actually took off, we were a jolly group of passengers, all orphans of the storm together. What began as camaraderie with my seatmate, an attractive man at least ten years my senior and also wearing a wedding ring, took on a flirtatious lilt, something I hadn't enjoyed for a very long time. Here I was in my new traveling dress, up in the turbulent air, unencumbered by children or husband. I felt glamorous. Desirable. Complete. When the pilot announced that the plane, now over three hours late, would be landing at Burbank, not LAX, my seatmate offered to share his cab with me. He, too, was headed for the Beverly Wilshire. I thanked him, surprised by the pleasant ripple of excitement.

"But I'll have to call my husband as soon as we land," I said, as if calling attention to Upton would somehow protect me from myself.

Upton picked up right away when I called from the terminal.

"Where are you?" His voice was thin, like a child's. "Oh, sweetheart, I've been so worried." He sounded as though he were almost in tears. But not angry and not drunk, either; amazing, since he had expected me to arrive at six, in time for a nice dinner together.

The doorman at the Beverly Wilshire helped me out of the cab, and I said good night to my new friend, wondering if I'd run into him again—hoping I would—and I followed the porter to the elevator. Upton surprised me in the hall, swept me up like an eager bridegroom, and led me to our fancy room. Champagne on ice stood next to the little round table where crustless club sandwiches waited under a silver dome on the white table-cloth. The enormous bed was turned down, and the windows were open to rustling palm fronds in the summery night.

Upton ushered me to an armchair. "I got you a present in Chicago." Eyes bright with anticipation, he placed in my lap a big box wrapped in Florentine paper and tied with a blue satin bow. Upton's signature wrapping; not a bit of Scotch tape anywhere.

"Go on, open it!"

The ribbon fell open with one tug of the ends, the heavy paper just as easily. Inside the box, in a nest of tissue paper, lay a carefully folded coat of beautiful black and ochre tapestry. I held the mandarin collar up to my neck and stood, letting the length of tapestry fall to my ankles. It was stunning. Then I noticed the hidden zipper that ran from the waist to the collar. Below the waist, the coat was curiously open. I looked at Upton, puzzled.

"That's not all." He pointed to the box.

Under another layer of tissue paper lay more tapestry. I held it up. Pants? No, shorts! "Shorts?"

"Hot pants!" said Upton, beaming. "They're all the rage. Perfect with your legs! Try everything on while I run you a bath." Upton filled my glass, and disappeared into the bathroom.

The hot pants and long coat could have been made for me. I looked terrific. Tomorrow I would get some sheer, silky panty hose to really show off my legs. I posed in the bathroom doorway, and Upton took me in, head to toe, pleased as punch.

"Perfect?"

"Perfect!" He grinned. "Now take it off and get in the tub."

I undressed, listening to the water run, and thought of the night nine years ago, right after Sarah was born, when my mother had come to New York for a week to "help with the baby." We hadn't wanted her to come, but we couldn't prevent her. At least she was staying at Joan and Peter's apartment and not with us. That morning, Mummy and Upton had had a stupid confrontation, provoked when she, having ignored his invitation to dinner, discovered at the last minute that he was no longer expecting her. She had been brittle and distant with me all day. Late in the afternoon, Upton wasn't home when she left, nor when she let herself back in a few minutes later, thin-lipped and livid.

"I wasn't going to tell you this, but God told me to." God was the fall guy for most of my mother's outrageous actions. I'm not sure when she started hearing voices; I think they came with menopause, possibly abetted by bourbon. She stared at me from the bedroom doorway, her eyes frozen in fury. "God told me I must tell you that you have married a liar. Upton. Is. A. Liar." She spat out each word like poison, then turned and left for good.

If I weren't a brand-new mother recovering from a Caesarean section, I might not have broken down. But I was worn-out. For five days Mummy had swept into our apartment on a tide of disapproval. Now on this, her final afternoon, she left me in tears. When Upton got home he tenderly listened while I, still sobbing, told him how awful she had been. He held me and stroked my head, and when I stopped for air, offered me his ironed handkerchief.

"Stay right there." He said this very gently. "Do not move. I have to pick something up at Gristedes."

A few minutes later, he was back. I heard the bathtub begin to fill, and caught a whiff of something fresh: lavender or rosemary. He helped me out of bed and into the fragrant, steamy bathroom. On the edge of the tub, lined up like sentinels, were four sweaty open bottles of imported beer, nectar to a nursing mother in 1963 and a far cry from the cheap quart bottles of Ballantine in the refrigerator.

He settled me in the deep, frothy tub, tucked an errant strand of hair behind my ear, and kissed my cheek. "Now, I want you to stay here until you've finished every drop of beer."

Upton was my ally, my comforter. He came in to add hot water and remove the empties and I smelled steak when he opened the door. Sip by sip, my mother's outburst receded.

Now, under very different circumstances at the Beverly
Wilshire, Upton ran the water for me again, sweetened it with
salts and fragrant oil, undressed me, helped me in, and handed
me my champagne flute. He washed me, rinsed me, dried me,
wrapped me in a big, soft robe, and led me to the table, where we
devoured every dainty triangle sandwich. And soon, very soon after that, he led me to bed. It was as if we had been apart for
months, for years.

It was almost noon when we awoke, barely time to make
love again and shower before Joe appeared in the lobby. We were
having lunch with him and H. N. Swanson, "Swanie," his agent,
who had represented Faulkner, Fitzgerald, and Raymond Chan-
dler as well as Joyce Carol Oates and Joe. Swanie was installed in
his usual booth at the Brown Derby, where I tried not to stare at
the famous people. Every now and then Upton would kick me
under the table and decorously point with his head toward Rich-
ard Widmark (whom I didn't recognize) and Rita Hayworth,
whom I did.

After lunch, the men had work to do and I went to the roof-
top pool at the hotel, stripped to my bikini. The L.A. sun felt
good on my winter-white skin. I thought briefly of the children
enjoying a snow day from school, and then my thoughts drifted
to the plane trip and my seatmate. Yesterday it had seemed like
such heady stuff, but now I didn't really care. I had Upton back,
and that was enough.

That night Dee, Joe's wife, came in from their house high in
the hills southeast of L.A. and we all had dinner at Chasen's,
where the doorman, maître d', and waiters knew Joe by name. I
wanted to wear my new hot pants, but decided to save them for
the big party the next night, where Joe said there'd be a band

and dancing. After dinner, we piled into Joe's new car (an all-black version of his black-and-white Ford police car) and went first to a Spanish bar with flamenco dancers and then to a Middle Eastern bar with belly dancers. These were not fancy Hollywood nightclubs where people went to be seen; these clubs were filled with Spaniards, Syrians, Lebanese. The air was dark and smoky, heavy with the lure of sex. At both places, Joe brought in an armload of his books from the trunk of the car to sign for the bartenders and hatcheck girls whom he'd known over the years. Joe might be a bestselling author with a new book and a new movie, but in these two clubs, Joseph Wambaugh was an LAPD cop, and he took good care of his friends on the beat.

The next day we checked out of the Beverly Wilshire and navigated the freeway east to the tawny hills where Joe and Dee and their two boys lived in a modest ranch, with open land and animals. The boys gave their bedroom to Upton and me, and I finally put on my new hot pants for the party. First Upton, then Joe looked me up and down, nodding, their eyes bright with approval. I felt as though I could conquer the world.

The noisy, exuberant party was given by Joe's LAPD partner and their colleagues. Tables were crowded with platters of couscous, garlicky cumin-scented lamb, stuffed grape leaves, bowls of hummus, minty yogurt, baba ghanoush—exotic fare I'd never tasted before in New England. And a full bar. Musicians played ouds, bouzoukis, mellow drums. People danced. No waltzes, fox-trots, or merengues. Another kind of dancing altogether, more elemental, men alone, men with men, women alone, belly dancing.

The music throbbed like blood and transformed itself into liquid motion. Hips, breasts, pelvises moving like rivers, waves all connected to a deep interior pulse. People clapped, swayed, cheered, but the dancers were not performing; they were dancing for themselves alone.

I wanted to do it, but this was no merengue with Upton. And so I merely watched, and let the music and the insistent rhythm move through me, loosening little muscles, until my hips made tiny circles and my shoulders fluttered. Upton didn't dance; he didn't even watch the dancing the way I did. He drank and ate and told stories. As Joe's publisher, he could stand a little apart. And he did.

Woman after woman—guests like me—belly-danced in their regular party clothes, no sparkly costumes with veils swirling around bare, beautiful, undulating midriffs. These dancers were wives, mothers, even grandmothers with bodies that had given birth and worked hard and that showed the progress of time. Their dancing was personal and intimate. There was no call for a partner, no need of a man.

The music stopped briefly, and I turned to the woman beside me. "I want to do that," I said.

"Then you must!" She gave me a playful push toward the dance floor.

"I can't." I shook my head. "I don't know how."

She smiled. "Everyone knows how."

The music started up again, and I watched another woman get up and slowly fill the space. When I got back to snowy Massachusetts, I would find someone to teach me—not the steps, not footwork, but how to unlock this part of myself.

We wound up our trip the next day in San Francisco, where Herb Caen in the *Chronicle* called us the toast of the town: "Affable Boston editor Upton Brady and his scintillating wife,

Sally . . ." There were two days of parties with San Francisco's elite, one for writer and muckraker Jessica Mitford and her husband, United States Communist Party chief Bob Treuhaft, where I also chatted with the president of Levi Strauss and the founder and curator of a curious waterfront museum. There was the book party for Madame Chiang, an elaborate banquet of many courses—smoked tea duck and beggar's chicken with Julia Child and M. F. K. Fisher. My last day in San Francisco, the museum curator, an attractive man maybe ten years my senior, invited me to visit his museum.

"It's on an old barge in the harbor," he said, with an easy charm. "Then lunch? Dim sum?"

"Dim sum?"

"You've never had dim sum?"

I'd never even heard of dim sum.

He said he'd take me to the airport after lunch, so Upton and I said our good-byes at breakfast, Upton flying back earlier by way of New York. It was another adventure all my own, like the plane trip out. I was Sally. Not Upton's wife or Sarah's mother. Just Sally. Someone I hadn't really spent much time with for the past ten years.

The museum was a collection of over a hundred years' worth of American packaging, which sounded odd when I heard about it, but which actually presented very telling and unexpected artifacts of social history—the first Campbell's soup cans, the first frozen food packages from Birds Eye. In Chinatown, we lingered over dim sum, unaware of passing time. It was very late when we left, speeding off to the airport in his polished, low-slung Jaguar XKE. He kept looking at his watch, and I'd feel the car surge ahead. We were close to the airport with minutes to spare and I thought I'd get my ticket out, ready for the dash to the plane. But when I opened the Pan Am envelope, it was empty. No ticket. I had checked the envelope that morning in the hotel room and my ticket to Boston had been right there. What could have happened? Never mind. What would I do now? I had no checkbook, and in 1972, no credit card. We were almost at the Pan Am entrance. I had to say something.

"My ticket isn't here," I said, feeling the flush spread up my neck.

"No ticket?"

"No ticket." I held my breath.

"Never mind, I'll get you one. That is"—he turned and grinned—"if they'll hold the plane." Could he be enjoying this whole drama?

He peeled up to the curb and leapt out of the car with my bag while I tripped along behind him in my little heels. He told Pan Am who he was and demanded they hold the plane. They did. He bought my ticket. I fled outside, where the plane sat on the tarmac. Someone wheeled the stairs back to the plane and the flight attendant opened the door. I gave my benefactor a quick wave and boarded. People stared while I took my seat. I put my new friend's card carefully in my wallet, thinking of the note I'd write to accompany my check for the ticket.

On the flight home, my seatmate was an over-friendly salesman who showed me pictures of his children and talked about his golf game. As soon as the seat belt light went off, he got up. "Going to play a little poker," he said.

"Poker? Where?"

"Up in the lounge."

I loved poker. After a while, I couldn't resist the temptation to check out the lounge, separate from the plane with its own bar and several big tables. Through a haze of smoke, I spied my seatmate sitting at one of them, with three other men, running the cards. Judging from the pile of bills, I guessed this was serious poker, and from the empty glasses, that the players were not entirely sober. I watched for a few minutes, itching to play. I still had a wad of bills in my wallet, unspent money that I'd budgeted for the trip. Why not?

"Don't you need a fifth?" All poker players know you can't get up a really good game with fewer than five.

The four men looked up at me, incredulous.

"You *play*?" asked my seatmate.

"I do," I said, sliding into the seat at the end.

"Five stud?" asked one of them, in a voice that implied I'd lose.

"Deal me in."

Everyone anted a dollar; this was going to be an expensive game. Maybe my only game, which probably would have made the others happy. I don't usually stick around where I'm not wanted, but the past few days had changed me; even the race to the airport had given me a dash of bravado.

Five stud is not for sissies, but Lady Luck was flying on Pan Am with me that night, and I drew a straight. The men were shocked, but assured one another that it was just beginner's luck, and it would change. But I steadily won hand after hand as most of the United States passed beneath me. Even though I lost three hands while the plane circled Boston, by the time we landed I had won over four hundred dollars, more than the cost of my lost plane ticket. And as it turned out, the ticket wasn't lost. Upton had pocketed it, mistaking it for his. He was very apologetic when I got home, but even so, I couldn't help thinking how completely lucky I had been, both winning at cards and ending up blameless in the missing ticket incident. If I had pocketed Upton's ticket, the outcome surely would have been different.

Once back, even though my days were much the same—filled with children, other mothers, chores, and animals—I began to carve out a more independent life. I started jogging very early before the little boys I took care of were dropped off and well before breakfast; I found a belly-dancing class in a neighboring town that even offered free babysitting; and best of all, when the children napped and on the weekends, I began to write.

Writing brought me solace and clarity. It satisfied the same urge to communicate that had made me want to perform on a stage and in time brought me a little money and recognition. I started by writing restaurant reviews for a glossy but short-lived magazine, *The Boston Review of the Arts*. In order to review the restaurants, we had to eat at them, and in order to taste many dishes, I would ask several friends to join us. The magazine paid for my words, but we each paid for our dinners, and it was a barely break-even arrangement. But it gave me a chance to eat out, something Upton and I practically never did together, not wanting to spend the money. And more important, it led to my first book, *Instar*, a dark novel published by Doubleday in 1976. It was reviewed by Margo Jefferson in *Newsweek,* and selected as the beach pick of the summer. Doubleday sprang for a full-page ad in *The New York Times Book Review,* it went into a second printing, and Ballantine bought the paperback rights.

Hugh, the narrator of *Instar,* is an alcoholic with a wife and four children. I hadn't meant to write the whole book from the point of view of a man, but I started writing in the first person, thinking it would help me get to know how my protagonist saw the world. And it did. Once I found his voice, I just kept going. I was Hugh while I was writing. His weaknesses were mine, as were his passions and his perceptions. And while Hugh was not Upton, they soon shared many qualities. As I explored Hugh, I also explored Upton. This was intuitive, not deliberate. Looking back, I am sure writing from Hugh's point of view led me through the growing tangle of thorns in my own marriage. Out of the blue, I invented a brother for Hugh, Omar, who was homosexual, as if I needed to explore this, too, although I never deliberately set out to do it.

Upton was proud of my success; he was my first reader, and I really learned to write through his sharp edits. He gave me ideas, interesting words. He even gave me the title: *Instar.* We talked about the content of the book, about the characters and the narrative arc and the dialogue. But we never discussed how the fictional marriage might relate to the actual marriage.

It took only a few years for Upton to run through Madee's inheritance. He didn't discuss it, he didn't go over the accounts with me, but when I asked him for extra money for back-to-school clothes, for instance, he would flare.

"Can't you understand there isn't any money?"

No money for children's shoes, but always enough for Upton's liquor; always enough for his cigarettes. I did what women have always done: figured out a way to stretch the food money to pay for the shoes. And I had what I earned from my two day-care tots. There was a high-end consignment store nearby that kept Sarah in Viyella jumpers and Liberty smocked dresses, and the boys in Izod polo shirts and corduroys. There was Marshalls for shoes, and seasonal boxes of expensive hand-me-downs in perfect condition from my sister. We not only managed, we managed to appear as well-dressed and well-housed as the landed gentry in neighboring Concord and Lincoln. I paid for the ponies' feed and the garden from my day-care money, which I knew Upton resented.

Fear has an insidious way of blossoming, once you let it in. I discovered that my protagonist, Hugh, like Upton, was given to volatile, alcoholic behavior. But Hugh was an invention. I was living day-to-day with Upton while I was exploring Hugh. I watched Hugh's drunken rampages intensify on the page and became more wary of crossing Upton. The self-assured independence I'd begun to enjoy since California was also leading me away from Upton, which gave me a little perspective. I did not want to confront him, and whenever I could step aside, I did. But not without resenting it, not without feeling silenced, not without a growing dissatisfaction and loneliness.

One day while I was writing, but a year before I actually sold my book and the last year of taking in other people's children, our landlady, who was also my friend, knocked at the door.

"Can I come in?"

Jane settled at the kitchen table with a cup of tea, gracious and smiling at the two little day-care boys zooming around on their Big Wheels, but I could tell she was worried about something.

"Did you know Upton is three months behind in the rent?"

Suddenly I was standing on the lip of Purgatory again, swallowed by fear, Upton lost from view. I said nothing, just stared back at Jane, holding on tight to the edge of the table.

She nodded. "I didn't think you knew. And that brings me to

the second reason for dropping in. His drinking." Her eyes held mine for a moment.

I knew Jane's husband was an alcoholic, a longtime member of AA. I knew that after twenty years, he still sometimes had "slips."

She took my hand. "Have you considered Al-Anon?"

"For me?" I got up, letting her hand drop. I thought Jane would suggest a plan for Upton, not one for me.

"For you. Al-Anon saved me while Joe was still drinking. I still go."

She told me about a group in nearby Waltham that met the next morning, and told me to call her any time at all if she could help.

"And about the rent—don't worry. Just take care of it when you can."

Confronting Upton on this would not be easy. I was afraid the rent might be merely the tip of a great, hidden iceberg. I decided to go to Al-Anon first, partly to postpone the scene with Upton, and partly because I hoped I'd find something there, some solace or a nugget of strength. I left the children with a neighbor and returned an hour later with a dawning clarity. I was not to blame for Upton's drinking. I was not guilty. He was sick. Not bad. Sick. I knew he was sick before I went to Al-Anon, but hearing so many others say it out loud was a crucial confirmation. Most important, I left the meeting knowing there was hope. Transformation was a phone call away.

That night after he settled in with his bourbon before dinner, I told Upton that Jane had come by, wondering what happened to the past three months of rent.

"Sally, this isn't the time to talk about it." His voice was querulous and patronizing—any moron could see this wasn't the right time to talk about it.

"Well, when would be a better time to talk about it?" How hard should I push? I didn't want to hear him say "*my* money." I didn't want him to explode. I didn't want him to burst into tears.

"Saturday morning." His words were flat and chilly.

Okay, Saturday morning it was. "Could you have all the unpaid bills for me to see?" At least I said this, even if my voice was shaky.

"If that's what you want." And Upton, thin-lipped, got up and busied himself with a refill of whiskey.

On Saturday morning I found out that the rent, though only one of the outstanding bills, was the greatest. That was a relief. I totaled up the debt, which came to $1,500. This seemed insurmountable in 1974. I looked at Upton's pay stubs, discovering for the first time in eight years exactly what his take-home pay was, and exactly where it went. Upton's budget was meticulous, but while it included cigarettes, it didn't mention liquor. Or lunches at the Ritz. Or clothes for anyone. No dentist, no drugs. But the budget could wait. First I had to pay the debt.

Madee had made me a special bequest of a thousand dollars, a substantial windfall at the time, really the first chunk of money I'd ever been given. I had put it in a savings account, thinking I would keep it, as Madee had hoped I would, for a trip to Europe. But that would have to wait; we needed the money now. I didn't want to spend it, but I didn't know what else to do. And it wasn't enough. Next, I called my sister Joan's husband, Peter. He was a banker in New York, the son and grandson of bankers. Peter was careful and kind, and I knew he could spare five hundred dollars. He said he would give me a loan, at a low interest rate, and that he would give me a schedule of payments, about forty-five dollars a month.

A few days later, when all this was settled and I had Peter's check and a draft from the bank, I made another appointment to talk to Upton. I told him I would pay the past debt, but that from now on, he would have to take what he needed for himself out of his paycheck and give me the rest. Period. I would pay the bills. This was nonnegotiable. He had to agree. There wasn't much talk. He seemed more angry than relieved when we finished, as if the unpaid bills were my fault. And the next day, when I told him all the bills were paid, Upton looked beaten, as though he had lost a great battle.

I think this was a turning point. After the confrontation about money, everything seemed harder for Upton. He had more trouble shrugging off Peter Davison's barbs, and his old zest for life lost some of its snap. I have wondered if Madee's death might have been a factor. Buff and Lucy were also having their own troubles. Buff began to disappear—he would just drop out for short stretches of time, not telling his wife, Mary, where he was and missing work. They separated for good a few years after Madee died. Buff didn't stick with any job for long, and was unreliable about paying child support. Fortunately for their two children, Mary had a secure position teaching at an excellent private school on the Upper East Side.

Lucy, the youngest of Upton's siblings, had been forced to leave the Catholic Church in 1969 when she married Bob, because he'd been previously married. Even though this was post–Vatican II, in the eyes of the Church, Bob was still married to his first wife. Madee had been just as enraged by this as the rest of us. When Madee died, Lucy was seven months pregnant with Amanda. Two years later, Bob and Lucy separated, leaving Amanda and Breezy, their eighteen-month-old foster child, with Upton and me for several months while Lucy sorted out her life, found a job and a new place to live in Washington, D.C. She ultimately returned Breezy to his father, enrolled in Virginia Theological Seminary, was ordained an Episcopal priest, and told us she was gay. Upton wrestled with Lucy's new life. First, he said he couldn't possibly go to her ordination.

"How can I receive the Eucharist in an Episcopal church? How can I accept it from the hands of a woman priest?" His anguish was honest.

But I, the infidel convert, couldn't accept this hocus-pocus. "Upton, do you really think God cares if the Eucharist is consecrated by a woman? Or an Episcopalian? Or a lesbian?"

In the end, he went. He received the sacraments from Lucy's tainted hands, even though he still didn't think it was right. When Lucy came to visit us, bringing Amanda, she also brought her partner, and while Lucy would always hold an unshakable place in his heart, he was very ill at ease with her new relationship.

"How can she be attracted to another woman?" Or "I just don't get it. How could she leave Bob for this?"

If Madee hadn't died at sixty-two, would all of these deep changes in her children's lives have happened when they did, and happened openly? Would they have happened at all? Madee was a powerful index of right and wrong, and had instilled in her children a lasting and urgent need for her approval. I think they resented her for this. I know Upton did. And after she died, he transferred his resentment for Madee to me. This was very clear in the whole sad episode of the unpaid rent.

Upton still had his projects, but they had evolved from play into work. His garden, an uncomplicated but showy border that ran along the front of a low brick porch, was the exception and a source of great pleasure. He kept the roses pruned and fed, cutting single stems of buds and blossoms for the living room, and reveled every May in the fluttering clouds of white bearded iris.

The house was old and in constant need of paint and patching projects that involved us both but which he masterminded. In return for a very low rent, we were supposed to take care of the upkeep, except for major expenses like the roof and the furnace. Upton kept the cars running as well, except for major problems. He found twenty-eight yards of English chintz on sale and whipped up lined and pleated curtains for the dining room; he wrestled bolts of discount corduroy and velvet into slipcovers for the down sofa and chairs that he'd originally found at the Salvation Army. But all this was work, and Upton was quick to say that he hated work.

In 1974, Upton was working on *The Harvard Lampoon Centennial Celebration,* a big coffee-table book published in 1976 and filled with the best and worst of *Lampoon* humor. This was a book Upton loved, because of the content and because of Marty Kaplan, then president of the *Lampoon* and editor of the anthology. Great perks came along with this book. One was the boisterous Brady Brunch held at the *Lampoon* castle one Sunday noon for Upton and me and all four children. Elliott Gould was there, and members of the *Lampoon,* undergraduates whose behavior was very like my children's. Andrew, eleven, distinguished himself by dancing on the mantel of the seven-foot baronial fireplace.

But the event of all events was the dinner in 1974 for John

Wayne following the *Lampoon*'s "Brass Balls Award" for Wayne's "outstanding machismo and penchant for punching people." Wayne arrived riding on the top of an armored personnel carrier manned by the "Black Knights" of Troop D, Fifth Regiment. The dinner was held in the Castle, a black-tie event for about thirty of us, mostly Harvard men. Even seated at the long refectory table, John Wayne was a giant. He was also very loud and very droll and held his own against the overeducated young Harvard men. The *Lampoon* served up its usual festive dinner of steak, baked potatoes, and salad. And a great deal of wine. When we had finished, someone turned on the music, and the Narthex or the Ibis of the *Lampoon* climbed from his chair onto the table, which was still littered with all the china and glasses from dinner. And then he began to kick plates, forks, wineglasses— sending everything within reach of his feet onto the tile floor. Soon everyone was up on the table, including John Wayne, kicking away, dirty crockery shattering while the music blared. For someone like me who spent many hours with a soapy dishpan, this was highly therapeutic.

As soon as the table was cleared, the dancing began. I was the smallest of the handful of women present, and I was the one the Duke chose to dance with. He was a monolith, heavily corseted, and very drunk. It was like dancing with a Roman column. His enormous belt buckle bit into my cheek; his hand covered my entire back. Every step was like thunder. And then, there were no steps. The Duke stopped dancing, and just leaned into me. Only he wasn't leaning, he was passing out. He was passing out on top of me. And then suddenly he was upright, in the arms of two bodyguards almost as big as he, who carried him away. That was my dance with the Duke.

About this time Upton latched on to a quote he loved and I hated, "Die now and avoid trouble later," saying it when he lighted up a Pall Mall or poured another drink or started coughing. His unattractive smoker's hack now occasionally erupted in spasms, making it impossible for him or anyone else in the room to carry on a conversation. The cough worried me at first, but then, over the years, I grew to despise it. When I was tired and grumpy, his coughing, like his colorful stories, seemed like just another way for him to control the conversation. And then I would feel guilty for being so unsympathetic. But I could see that his cough, like his drinking, separated Upton from everyone around him. I wanted to cry out, "Stay here, with us!" but I don't think he could have heard me because by then he was already too far away.

VERMONT, APRIL 18, 2008

Seven-year-old Max comes with me to the probate court this bright morning, his hand in mine as we climb the stairs. His three-year-old brother, Zachary, is snoozing in his car seat, and Sarah has a book to keep her company while I reveal the state of Upton's finances to the probate clerk and wait to find out what my next step is. Afterward, we'll take our picnic and hike up Mt. Tom, where fillets of snow still linger in the woods. I've been instructed to bring Upton's death certificate and his will, in addition to his recent bank statements and bills, to the probate office. I hand the folder to the friendly clerk and then sit down with Max. Seventy thousand dollars. How can I ever climb out of this hole? It doesn't take the clerk long to reappear at the counter.

"This is certainly a matter for probate," she says, returning my folder. "Shouldn't be any problem. Since almost all these bills are in his name only, and since he had no assets, there is no estate."

She goes on to explain the extensive and ongoing paperwork I'll have to attend to through September or October, when the case will actually come before the court. Of the fourteen accounts, only three are not eligible: an old joint bank account with an outstanding credit line that I have never used and until a few days ago had forgotten existed; a maxed-out credit card jointly in Upton's and Alex's names that Upton had taken out twenty years ago for Alex, who, at sixteen, was studying ballet in New York; and a business credit card for which I am also responsible. In keeping with Upton's rule of "*my* money," all his other credit cards and bank accounts, which total just over $60,000, are in his name only and have nothing to do with me.

My money. I find this reminder of Upton ironic and at the same time I feel tears threaten behind my eyes. Did he have any idea that this might absolve me from his debt? I would like to think he did. I would like to believe that the reason Upton kept his finances to himself was to keep me free of his debt. But I don't believe it.

The clerk gives me a reassuring half smile. "Make sure you let all the creditors know this is going to probate. And don't make any payments."

I summon the courage to ask her if she believes this will be approved, and all the debt erased.

"There are no assets," she repeats, kindly. "If there is no money, how can the debts possibly be met? Don't worry, it will be all right."

I remember Alex at seventeen, coming to Upton in tears when he had overspent his budget.

"Alex," said Upton, his voice surprisingly calm and tender, "money comes and money goes. But never get emotional about it. Always, always remember, money is only money."

I take Max's hand and step out into the April sun.

6

*Don't turn your head. Keep looking at the
bandaged place.
That is where the light enters you.*

—HAFIZ

VERMONT, JUNE 2008

Spring is giving way to summer—how can this be? How can there
be a new grandchild, Henry, now a week old, whom Upton will
never meet? How can there be roses and strawberries when there
was deep snow just yesterday when Upton and I held hands and
shared our soup? Just yesterday, when Upton died. Three months
ago, actually. I can't seem to let go of finding the pornography; I
question our marriage over and over again, wondering how he
could have made love to me for all those years when what he really
wanted was a male lover. How could he have worked so hard to
stay married to me? Where did Upton put his gay life when we
prayed together at Mass, and shared the kiss of peace? Where
was it when he meditated every morning? Archbishop Rembert
Weakland, a leading liberal Roman Catholic whom we met several years ago, has been in the news lately for admitting he has had
sex with consenting men. He said the Roman Catholic Church

teaches that homosexuality is "an objective disorder." He went on to say that he had had relationships with other men because "of loneliness that became very strong." Did my objectively disordered husband suffer from "loneliness that became very strong"?

The permanence of Upton's death has solidified in the wake of the searing, immediate shock, but I'm buffeted by sparring questions: Did Upton know how much I loved him; did I show him every day? Did he love me, love waking up beside me every morning, or did he long for another kind of life with another kind of person? Until lately, I had trusted that Upton loved me with a rare and loyal passion, in spite of his deep anger, in spite of everything. Even when our marriage was at its most fragile and darkest point, I was sure that if the marriage were to end, I, not Upton, would be the one to deliver the severing blow. So why do I question his love now, when his roses are in full bloom and the days are long?

On Mother's Day I worked in the garden from morning well into the afternoon when I suddenly realized that Upton hadn't called from the front steps "How about a rum punch?" as he always did on summer weekends. Today, I snip three pale pink buds from his Dr. Van Fleet rosebush and put them in the small pitcher in the center of the table, as he would have done. Every weeknight dinner, each hand-squeezed lime in my rum punch, every Glenn Gould Goldberg Variation on the CD player after dinner, every shared article from *The New York Review of Books*, or deliberately recalled antic from his noonday forays, all of these were acts of Upton's love. How can I doubt it? But I do. I think of the gleaming naked men, I think of Edward, I think of all the intervening years between these discoveries, and I despair.

People ask me if I'm healing. Healing? Why should I heal? What's wrong with rupture? *Living with Rupture*—sounds like the title of a best seller to me. I've been reading books lately about losing spouses, by Joan Didion, Nora Ephron, Donald Hall, plus a few how-to's on widowhood, and I'm getting a little fed up with everyone's trying to avoid self-pity. Why not indulge in self-pity? If not now, for goodness sake, then when? Actually, I've become a welcome wagon for both Self-Pity and her more important brother, Grief. The three of us are thicker than thieves.

"Come right in," I say. "The guest room is all ready—linen sheets, fresh flowers, truffled rack of lamb for dinner with my only bottle of Château Mouton Rothschild. Make yourself at home!"

Aren't I afraid that with such hospitality Self-Pity and Grief will move in for good? No, I expect they'll begin to bore me, as lingering guests usually do. I will stop ironing the pillowcases and start serving up tuna casseroles. Self-Pity will certainly soon pack up and move on. Heaven knows there are plenty of people with empty guest rooms all made up for her, and a place set for her at tables everywhere. As Upton used to say: "Self-pity is like wetting your pants in winter—it feels very good for a very short time."

I need to step back, get some perspective. I decide to go to New York. For one thing, I badly need a haircut, always an excellent reason to go to New York. I also want to meet with two of Upton's writers to talk about the future, and with several editors to discuss manuscripts. It will be salubrious to get out of this little house of memories for a few days, stay with my sister at the Union Club, a relatively Upton-free zone with no shirts to sniff in the closet, no labels on freezer packages in his unmistakable hand, no harassing calls from persistent creditors. Getting away might break the loop of doubt as well. Doubt has become my new preoccupation.

A week after Upton died, my cell phone rang, most unusual as there isn't reliable reception up here in the mountains. After I took the call, I saw there was also a missed message. From Upton, left the day before he died. Everything is present in his voice, a gladness in the greeting, enthusiasm (he is replying to a message I left for him about having sold a book), the worrisome breath before each new phrase and the even more worrisome cough.

I want to say there is a lovingness in that voice, too. Not the racing, eager passion of new love, but the ripe kindness and welcome familiarity that only come with time. When the message is over I play it again, and again. I can't get enough of it. There are options offered at the end, including one to return the call, which makes me sob out loud as I sit in the car pressing *replay*. I listen to the options: seven to delete; nine to save. But only for twenty-one days. So I listen to Upton every day. Will I always do this? Will there be a day, a whole week, when I forget? Will I miss one of those twenty-first days when I have to renew the message or lose it forever?

In the six weeks of my father's dying, his blue eyes were often closed, which gave him a peaceful look but reminded me that I was on the outside and removed from his suffering. One clear September morning on my way to the hospital, I realized that the sky was the exact color of Daddy's eyes. This gave me a wonderful jolt of recognition, a visceral connection to my almost comatose father. He died that night. Yet even now, fourteen years later, I still see his eyes in that particular blue of the sky.

This morning, as I look across the meadow to Mt. Ascutney, the sky near the horizon is a different blue from the deep of its dome, paler with a brush of aqua. Upton's eyes. Here I am, almost three months after his death, listening to his voice and finding him just above the horizon. Tomorrow I go to New York.

BEDFORD, 1975–1980

In a family soccer game with five-year-olds and pregnant mothers the Sunday after Thanksgiving, 1975, Upton and another father collided. Upton fell to the ground, unconscious, the wind knocked out of him. I knelt beside him, surrounded by a huddle of worried friends. His usually rosy face was chalky. Nothing moved. He looked dead. Then his lips parted and air came out, a prolonged, steady, and foul-smelling exhale that went on so long I thought it might have been his very last breath. And then there was no breath at all for what seemed like forever. Finally, he opened his eyes. They were cloudy and his face was like gray putty, but Upton knew where he was.

"I'm fine." He struggled to his feet and, once up, to keep his balance. "No ER; just take me home."

And I did, knowing that something was very wrong. Once home, I called Ben, our internist next-door neighbor, who checked Upton out and then asked me in private if Upton was lucky.

"Lucky?" I thought of Upton's life so far: honors from Harvard, managing editor of Atlantic Monthly Press, four beautiful children, me. I thought of the many drunken drives home and his safe return. Yes, Upton was lucky. Still, it made me uneasy to hear a respectable Boston doctor talk about luck. "What does luck have to do with it?"

Ben shrugged his shoulders. "I find that people who have good luck in their lives tend to have good luck medically."

Perhaps there is truth in this.

Ben then gave me a list of symptoms to look out for, and told me that if any of them occurred I should take Upton directly to the ER. Internal bleeding was one, and within a few hours, Upton announced in a worried voice that there was blood in his urine. He spent from Thanksgiving Sunday until New Year's Eve in Emerson hospital. One of his kidneys had been badly damaged, and he was in severe pain for several weeks while he passed huge blood clots. But even in pain, the first thing Upton did when he rolled off the gurney from the ER onto the bed in his room was to light a cigarette. The second thing was ask me to bring him a bottle of bourbon to keep in his bedside cupboard. When the urologist came in I asked him if bourbon was a good idea, and in front of Upton he said no. So that was settled.

But there was nothing I could do about the cigarettes; not only was smoking allowed in hospitals in 1975, you could even give the nurse's aide $1.25 and she'd buy you a pack of Pall Malls in the cafeteria. I stopped Dr. Trinkler in the hall the next day and begged him to forbid Upton to smoke.

"If you tell him he can't," I said, "he won't. It's a golden opportunity."

Dr. Trinkler gave me an incredulous look. "I can't do that," he said.

"Why not?" (This was years before any mention of patients' rights.)

"Upton's smoking isn't my business."

"Isn't his health your business?"

"His kidney is my business."

A few days later, I ran into Dr. Trinkler in the cafeteria, lighting up.

As Christmas drew closer, I struggled to juggle the demands of the fast-approaching holidays with daily trips to the hospital. In keeping with Church tradition, Advent was a penitential season, a kind of mini-Lent with its own family rituals. Every night the children and I read a Christmas story together and added the relevant Nativity figure to the twenty-four piece crèche; we baked and decorated dozens of cookies, polished the brass and silver, and hung wreaths and garlands on the doors and windows. I tried to do everything exactly as we would if Upton were home, but it was hard to fit everything in, along with two daily visits to the hospital, twenty minutes away.

Upton, now sober and in less pain, was also growing restive and depressed. It is hard for a whirlwind of activity to suddenly have nothing to do. One day on a whim I stopped at the yarn shop and picked up knitting needles and wool. When I handed him the bag, Upton looked suspicious. He never liked surprises. But when he saw the wool, he immediately shifted gears, and the old eager light returned to his eyes.

"Hats! I'll make everyone a hat. Maybe mittens! Or a scarf!" And he went right to work, astonishing the nurses.

"Where did you learn to knit?" they'd ask.

"Mother's knee and other joints," he'd say, needles clicking.

As soon as he started his first striped hat, Upton's spirits began to lift, but mine didn't, with the chances of his coming home for Christmas diminishing day by day. Most of our family rituals at Christmas came from the Bradys—lighting the candle that carried its flame over six generations from Ireland; reading from the Gospel according to Luke; kneeling together for a silent prayer before bed. A few came from my family, like opening presents one by one instead of diving in all at once, opening only stockings before breakfast. And then there were the ones Upton and I dreamed up together: decorating the tree after the children had gone to bed on Christmas Eve; waking them at ten-thirty and traipsing off to Midnight Mass (which really did take place at midnight back then); and on Christmas morning, checking the display of unwrapped presents and bulging stockings in the living room, lighting the fire, and walking through the children's rooms on Christmas singing "Hark! The Herald Angels"— the signal for them to come downstairs, lining up in front of the living room door, youngest to oldest.

This year, without Upton to help us, I decided not to wait until Christmas Eve to put up the fifteen-foot tree and decorate it as we always had, and instead to get it done early. Lucy called to say she was coming alone (it was Bob's year to have Amanda for Christmas), which was a great comfort. I'd never set up a tree before and was worried that I might not do it right, but with Lucy to help, maybe we could. Having it up would be a big relief and might brighten our spirits as well as the living room. Andrew, ten, and Sarah, eleven, helped wrestle the big tree into the stand and tighten the screws into the trunk. We heaved it upright, and it stayed there, standing tall if a little crooked. If it was backed into the corner, no one would ever notice. Then came the lights, three hundred tiny white ones carefully placed so the wires didn't show. This always took forever, and the very idea used to drive Upton crazy. All four children helped with the ornaments. When we were done, we turned off the living-room lights and stood in the dark around the starry, bright tree. There was a palpable lifting of our spirits.

That Christmas, of all the children, I worried most about eight-year-old Natty, my sturdy, stalwart middle son. Each night when I got home from the hospital I would tuck in the children and bring them a nugget of news from Upton. And each night Natty would ask the same question.

"Pa will be home for Christmas, won't he?"

Natty liked having a dependable order to his days, and was even more relieved than I when the tree was done.

To celebrate our triumph with the tree, Lucy and I took the children out for hamburgers and ice cream and then to the hospital, where they told Upton all about it. I didn't bring them every day—it was tiring for Upton and sometimes hard for the children—but this visit was happy, and short. On the way home, we cruised the neighborhoods with the most lavish displays of lights, rating them with hubba-hubbas. We couldn't wait to turn into our own driveway and see our tree twinkling in the dark house. But when we pulled into the driveway, there was not a twinkle to be seen. The tree was on the floor, surrounded by shards of broken ornaments. Natty was the most despairing of us all.

I called one of the many kind friends who had offered help after Upton's injury, and twenty-four hours later, the tree was securely up, the lights and unbroken ornaments back on, and we were rolling out the cookies. But Natty wasn't reassured. The next day we found out that Upton could not come home.

"But how can we have Christmas without Pa?" sobbed Natty. "Who will light the candle? Who will get the fire going in the morning? Who will start the singing?"

Christmas without Upton wasn't the same, that's true. But we all remember the striped stocking hats, bright pennants in the bare, antiseptic hospital corridor. That was the day the old light returned to Upton, a look of accomplishment and pleasure as young as the children's when he handed them their presents, unmistakably wrapped by him with real satin ribbon and jewel-like paper. He looked like himself for the first time in four weeks—even younger than himself, his cheeks newly pink, his eyes their old clear blue, unclouded by pain or whiskey.

However, on New Year's Eve, after five weeks in the hospital, the urologist was still not sure he would be able to save Upton's kidney.

"Go home; give it six months," he said. "And see how it goes."

In June, a month after *Instar* was published, Upton had his kidney removed. He was in the hospital six days, and had been home for two when he very suddenly spiked a fever of 104, an allergic reaction to penicillin. We sped back to the hospital, where for five days he lay in intensive care on a refrigerated rubber sheet, trembling and comatose, his fever hovering around a hundred and four. His beard turned white, his skin pallid and desiccated. I watched my thirty-eight-year-old husband turn into an old man. In front of the children I tried to be as positive and hopeful as possible, but driving back and forth to the hospital, I was awash with tears. Cars are perfect, private capsules for despair.

The evening of the fifth day, the fever broke and Upton opened his eyes.

"Welcome back, Mr. Brady!" The nurse's sigh was as deep as my own. "We thought we'd lost you!"

Upton continued to drink every day, but he wasn't always drunk. He published a stunning array of books, from the centennial anthology of the Harvard Lampoon in 1976 to William Warner's Pulitzer Prize–winning *Beautiful Swimmers*. He worked with Abe Burrows on *Honest, Abe*, Burrows's autobiography, winding up each session with a rollicking lunch at Café des Artistes. When Agnes de Mille was writing her book about Lizzie Borden, Upton accompanied her to Fall River, and in the front hall of the ninety-year-old daughter of Lizzie's lawyer was handed a brown paper bag filled with Mrs. Borden's blood-encrusted hair and stained pillowcases. He escorted renowned movie critic Pauline Kael to the Ritz for lunch, and they were banned from the dining room because Kael was wearing a denim pantsuit. "It's Bill Blass, for Christ's sake!" hissed Pauline. Upton persuaded Nino, the maître d', to give them a secluded table behind a potted palm where Pauline's denim trousers and colorful language might both go unnoticed.

Erudite, intrigued by elegant new ideas, and still spilling over with boyish charm and humor, by 1977 Upton had made a name for himself in publishing and became director of the Atlantic Monthly Press.

His colleagues were aware of his drinking—I remember two separate afternoons when someone from work drove him home to Bedford after too many martinis at lunch—but most of the time Upton was careful not to cross the line between tipsy and falling-down drunk. He had the well-honed Brady work ethic, and was far more circumspect with authors, agents, and Atlantic colleagues than when he was at home with me. He was careful at work in the same way he was careful at sea. These were life-or-death pursuits.

For a number of years, we chartered a small, venerable sloop from friends for a week of cruising between Nantucket and Newport, and one year, we chartered a forty-foot Concordia yawl. Once he was aboard a boat, Upton carefully monitored his drinking and stayed alert. Even after we climbed into our bunks at night, he would remain watchful, sensitive to the slightest change in the anchor, wind, or sea. I would wake to find his berth empty, poke my head through the hatch, and find him checking the set of the anchor, or the swing room in a crowded harbor. Or just smoking in the stern, beneath a dome of summer stars. He was captain, in charge, our safety in his hands. On a boat, I think this responsibility felt right and good. We were self-contained, as if he held us in the palm of his hand. He made the rules, and we obeyed them, trusting him to bring us all safely home.

But once we were home, the world intruded, adding confusion to his disparate responsibilities. Often he didn't have any idea what we were all up to. Soccer, piano lessons, ponies, ballet, sleepovers, birthday parties—the changing kaleidoscope of busy children assembled and reassemble around him. We were busy, disorganized, messy. We didn't always put things back where they belonged, and important things like wrenches or sewing scissors or the little gizmo that measures tire pressure would temporarily stray, and Upton would explode. He couldn't navigate the ever-changing topography of the refrigerator or the pantry, or always objectively respond to the unpredictable, spontaneous demands of four growing children and their friends. Most of the time, he tried to be polite and, if possible, to inject a scrap of witty humor.

The safest way for Upton to respond to any new situation was to find a story to anchor him. Even when he'd had too much to drink, he could take a deep breath and slide into a story as easily as Spalding Gray or Noël Coward. Even when we'd heard the stories over and over again, Upton would catch us and we'd listen, riveted, while he anchored himself in the comfort of words. And of course, guests, young and old, were charmed. Sometimes, instead of cursing, Upton would indite a note, like this one, written when there were four adolescents sharing the shower with him, each with a different complement of toiletries jostling for space on the shelf. *"On those who leave the tops off shampoo bottles, I send an endless plague of axolotls!"*

Visitors had always streamed in and out of our houses, ever since those early New York days. Now, with a houseful of teen-aged children, there were simply more visitors, some staying a few hours, and some a few days, or weeks. This felt right to me, but looking back, I think it was hard for Upton. With guests, he had to keep his mercurial and alcohol-related moods in check; home was as unreliable as quicksand, and far more frightening than being in charge of a major publishing company or navigating a small sailboat in heavy seas.

When Upton lost his kidney, he also lost his hollow leg. The three-martini lunches became two-martini lunches with the same inebriating effects, and the nights of whiskey, wine, and more whiskey were now whiskey, wine, and less whiskey. Almost gone was the ever-narrowing window when a drink or two would relieve his psychic pain but not yet turn him into an angry, irra-tional drunk. Upton would slide from hungover to drunk in less than an hour. I began to notice occasional gaps in his memory, small ones that he was adept at covering up. At the time I thought it was simply inattention that made him unaware of day-to-day family trivia, but later I learned that these gaps were caused by blackouts. But the change in Upton that scared me most was the way his verbal abuse intensified as his tolerance for alcohol dwindled. No matter what he was really angry about, I was the target. I watched his hands clench and open and clench, afraid that at any moment, his verbal abuse might turn swiftly physical.

When Upton was sober and not hungover, when he was fully

present to me, we slipped back into a shared life. I knew he was proud of my success as a writer, proud of his children, proud of his own literary success. We laughed at the same silly jokes and relished juicy intellectual tidbits and quirky stories. These bright moments flickered in and out of the encroaching shadow of Upton's drinking and anger, and the darker causes that fueled them. Thanks to Al-Anon, I was beginning to believe that I was not the cause of Upton's drinking; I was learning to step back.

On the Saturday before Mothers Day, 1977, a week before Upton and I were leaving for two weeks in Europe, Buff called. He and Mary had been separated for about a year, and we hadn't really been in touch. Once in a while Mary would call, complaining that she didn't know where Buff was, that he hadn't seen the children or was late with his check, but Upton hadn't wanted to get involved. The rift between him and Buff that split wide open when Madee died had never healed.

I was making breakfast when the phone rang, and I was happy to hear Buff's voice. But he sounded far away and uncertain.

"Where are you?" I asked, hearing a PA announcement in the pause before he answered.

"Bellevue," he said.

"Bellevue! Are you okay?" He couldn't be, not if he was in Bellevue Hospital. In 1976, it was akin to bedlam. Filthy, overcrowded, understaffed—no one would willingly check into Bellevue. Buff said the police had picked him up off the street the night before. He'd blacked out.

"They're letting me out tomorrow."

I waited for him to say where he was going. Silence.

"Where will you go?" Since he'd left Mary, we hadn't had a permanent address for him.

"I don't know. That's why I'm calling."

Buff had no place to live. How was this possible? "Do you want to come here?" The words flew out of my mouth.

It never occurred to me to ask Upton if Buff could come. Or to ask Buff how long he planned to stay. I told Buff we'd meet the one o'clock train the next day, praying he'd find the money for a ticket.

When I told Upton, he was immediately concerned for Buff, aghast that he was in Bellevue. But then he asked me how long Buff was planning to stay, and I had to tell him I didn't know.

"Does he have a job? An apartment?" Upton's questions came like bullets.

"I don't know. I don't think so."

"That's what I'm afraid of. He has no place to go." Upton sighed. "He'll be here forever."

"Upton, it's an emergency! He doesn't want to live with us; he just needs time to pull himself together."

The next morning after Mass we drove to the station, forty minutes from home. It was a beautiful spring day, and this felt like an excursion. We'd all tidied up the little spare room for Buff; the bed was made, the children excited. I didn't know what condition Buff would be in after Bellevue, or how wasted he might be from drugs, in addition to booze. He was thinner and paler than usual, but still handsome and funny. I didn't know until Upton opened the trunk of the car that he had packed a shaker of martinis and two glasses, and I was sickened when he placed the glass in Buff's trembling hand before we even left the station. This gesture of hospitality and brotherly kindness may have shocked me, but it delighted Buff. The warning was plain, yet I missed it, absorbed in the rescue, not in the cause of the crisis. And I was relieved that Upton seemed happy Buff had come.

A week later, we left Buff and the children with the babysitter and flew to London for a few days and then on to France and Italy. Most of my advance for *Instar* had gone toward paying off all our bills and buying a new car. But I kept some money to go to Europe. Before Upton and I were married, I longed to have him show me the places he'd loved so much when he went abroad in 1958. He had told me a lot about Rome—a Piranesi etching of the Piazza di Spagna and the Trinità dei Monti hung above our bed. He had told me stories about hitchhiking to Avignon, and sleeping on the field at Runnymede. I thought he would be eager to return, and grateful for his free trip.

But when I spread out the maps in February, and showed him my three new Guides Michelin, he balked.

"You should go to Europe on your own. Alone." His voice was patronizing, as though I were a dim child. As though it were unnatural, unreasonable, for a wife to want to travel abroad with her husband.

"Alone?" I felt spurned. Unloved. I thought I might burst into tears. "But I don't want to go alone. I want someone to share this with. I want to go with *you*!"

For the next month, Upton stalled, bringing up one lame excuse after another. I started to feel as though I were asking a great favor, instead of offering a great gift. And then something else kicked in, too. A stubborn determination to pry Upton away from his patterned life, away from his routine of work, away from his routine of drink. I wanted to shake Upton up. Not only that, I wanted to win. Finally, Upton agreed to go, though he made it seem like a sacrifice, not a treat. That did not keep me from dreaming about the trip, and making plans.

We would spend four nights in a modest London hotel with a shared bath, where Upton would meet with British authors and I would meet my Ballantine U.K. editor and marketing person. We would go to Hampshire to see writer Peter Dickinson, and to Winchester to meet Millie, an eighteen-year-old who would spend a year in the U.S. as our au pair before going on to Oxford. Then, overnight from Portsmouth across the channel to Calais. I reserved a stateroom for this, thinking it would be a romantic crossing but not taking into account that it was Pentecost weekend, when the ship would be overrun with French tourists.

In Calais, a Renault would be waiting and we would have a completely unplanned week driving through France, spending the night in whatever little town we ended up in. I wanted to explore Brittany, Le Mont-Saint-Michel, and the Loire Valley, especially Chinon. I knew Upton was eager to go to Burgundy and Lyons, and I thought we could spend a few days on the Riviera before heading on to Italy by train. We had our TTP tickets, and I'd made hotel reservations in Florence. Ann Cornelisen, author of *Torregreca* and, the year before, *Women of the Shadows*, was expecting us for a few nights in her stone house in a Tuscan olive grove. The last stop was Rome, where we would spend five nights at the top of the Spanish Steps, right next to the four-star Hassler.

The only unplanned part of the trip was the week in France, which excited me the most. In May there wouldn't be a problem finding places to stay, and to me, the idea of driving through a village and deciding on the spot to stay there had tremendous appeal. I had no idea how much Upton would despise traveling without an itinerary or reservations until we got off the boat in Saint-Malo. He'd had a lot to drink crossing the channel the night before, and was badly hungover at dawn, when the boat docked.

"Where's the car?" He thumbed through the folder of travel documents. "Where's the receipt from Hertz?" He was sweating on this cool, foggy morning, in a panic.

"Here's the reservation, and look! There's the car!" It was all just as it should have been. I wished he'd cheer up.

Upton scowled and slid into the driver's seat without a word. I thought of saying something—like "Hey, it's my car! Why don't you let me drive?" But I knew it would only make matters worse to usurp what little control he had over this trip. No point in fanning the already smoldering coals.

But things got worse anyway when Upton could not start the car. The engine growled but didn't turn over. He tried again and again, his face dark with fury.

I looked across to the dashboard, thought I saw a choke. "Maybe you need to use the choke," I ventured, not really knowing much about engines.

Upton gave me a blistering look. "It doesn't have a choke." He got out of the car and slammed the door. "I'm going to call Hertz." And he stomped off.

By then it was about seven-thirty, the day hardly begun. I doubted he would rouse anyone at Hertz, but it was good to have him gone for a few minutes. I got out of the car, climbed into the driver's seat, and gently pumped what looked like a choke button in and out a couple of times. Then I turned the key. The Renault started right up. Upton heard the noisy little engine from across the parking lot and turned, perhaps more furious with my success than he had been with his own failure. This was hardly an auspicious beginning to our drive through France.

I wanted to go to Europe mainly because I had never been. But I also wanted to go because I thought traveling with Upton might give me new insight. Our jaunt to California had given me such hope, both in my marriage and in myself. But in the ensuing five years, we seemed to have grown at different rates, and in different directions.

Upton seemed tired and removed from the children and me. I knew this was partly the isolation of alcohol, and partly the daily grind of work. Maybe this trip would shake something loose, and bring back the charming and curious Upton. Maybe in a new place, he would tip his head back and let his laughter spill and indulge his irreverent, maverick sense of humor. Jolted out of his routine, maybe Upton would recover his buoyancy.

And if he didn't? At least I would climb to the heights and depths of Mont-Saint-Michel and wait for the tide to cover the silty flats. I would skirt venerable Norman orchards and feel the heat of Calvados on my tongue. I would listen to Mass in lilting French while I marveled at the way the ancient bricks could arrange their angular shapes into graceful arches. I would discover that up close, the Loire seemed far too shallow for the great châteaux that studded its banks. No matter Upton's mood, I planned to fill myself right up with new sights and sounds and tastes and smells. With any luck, Upton might join me.

Sometimes he did. Mornings were good; he was most relaxed then, and open. We would buy bread, cheese, *fraises,* and a bottle of local wine, discover parks, riverbanks, or ramparts for our picnic, but as the shadows lengthened, Upton would become restive. I loved flipping through the Guide Michelin for little-known hamlets where we could spend the night. While I read the description of the lakeside pension aloud, I imagined the water shimmering in the morning sun.

"I want to know if there's a place to eat, not if there's a lake. I want to know if I'll have a bed to sleep in, for Christ's sake!"

A bed? A place to eat? No. A drink. It was the drink that made his destination so urgent.

Upton wasn't irritated; he was terrified. Back home, he used to say that the reason my mother never trusted anyone was that she didn't trust herself. Now it was clear: Upton didn't trust himself. How could he possibly trust me? He didn't want to travel without a plan, or even start the day without a schedule. What to me was a week of glorious free-form wandering must have been Upton's worst nightmare. There was no framework to hold him in. Where would he be when he woke up, today? Where would he sleep tomorrow? When, *when* could he have a drink?

On May 26, driving the hilly Burgundian country roads with ranks of vineyards on the southern slopes, Upton told me he had a birthday surprise for me, reservations in Montrachet, close to my favorite vineyard. I expected a stone country house with an airy room, darned linen pillowcases on the sagging horsehair mattress, a chipped china ewer on the walnut dresser, and an ancient bathroom down the hall. Instead, he proudly pulled into an asphalt wasteland surrounded by tidy vineyards, where a French version of Howard Johnson's presided. For Upton, the pièce de résistance of these familiar, bland accommodations was the gleaming, private bathroom and shower, with limitless scalding water, just like at any motel back home.

A restaurant next to the office served up simple food on Formica tables, not exactly my idea of a festive place for a birthday dinner in France. But the "local" wine, as it was called, more than made up for the pedestrian food and ambience. We were *les Américains,* an oddity in what was clearly a very French, very bourgeois motel. At our neighboring table, a grandmother and grandfather kept an eye on their ten-year-old grandson's manners and discussed their trip south, to the Riviera, where we, too, were headed.

Though not nearly as good as my misleadingly fine accent, my French was now good enough that I could understand and be understood most of the time. I asked *Grand-mère* to recommend a village near a beach and far from tourists. They were going to Saint-Raphaël, *"Mais,"* said *Grand-mère,* throwing up her hands, *"Saint-Raphaël a beaucoup de touristes et des hotel grands!"* Go to Fréjus Plage, said Grandma, no big hotels or tourists there, just family pensions near the beach. That night, lying on the giant king-size bed in the drone of the air conditioner, Upton having had his second shower in four hours, I decided that from now on, there would be no more one-night stands or last-minute decisions. We would spend our last three nights in Fréjus Plage whether we liked it or not.

The streets beside the Fréjus Plage beach ran in a grid, with similar small bungalows evenly placed with little room on either side—hints of Levittown but recently developed, with no big trees or lush gardens. There was barely grass. We parked the car and decided to look around on foot for a possible place to stay, each of us thinking we would probably be better off driving on to Saint-Raphaël. Purely by luck, Upton spotted the sign almost obscured by rampant clematis: IL ETAIT UNE FOIS—Once Upon a Time. The house itself was hidden from the street by a lush garden that ran through a thicket of fruit trees and arbors already heavy with grapes. We followed the curving, narrow path to the house, almost invisible in its camouflage of lichen-speckled stones and faded louvered shutters. The garden air was heavy and sweet and I felt as though we were indeed entering a fairy tale where anything might take place.

This was the first season for the young French family who ran the pension and small restaurant. They were surprised to see Americans and gave us their best corner room with ironed linen sheets worn thin and soft on the magisterial Victorian bed. We had our own marble sink and bidet, and a tiny balcony nestled in the treetops.

Every mouthful of the simple food that came from the kitchen of the pension was perfect, and we quickly switched from the plan that included only breakfast to the one that included lunch and dinner as well. The chef (an uncle of Monsieur le Patron) waved to us from the open kitchen door when we came in. The sous-chef was his eleven-year-old son, who welcomed us the last night proudly holding a large, still wriggling fish, which he had scooped just for us from the brook behind the kitchen. We ate what they served us, drank the wine on the table. Upton didn't mention whiskey. Every day we walked hand in hand on the nearly empty beach and swam in the very salty Mediterranean. On Sunday, we explored the big town of Fréjus after Mass in the cathedral. For three days we rested with each other. Even Upton's cough, which had been become a problem at night, seemed to subside.

Italy was easier. We had an itinerary, reservations, and no car to worry about. By the time our trip was over, Upton spent more time looking at the world around him than at the minute hand of his watch. Besides Florentine leather wallets, striped Roman silk scarves, and tiny nativity figures from Provence, I brought home a new understanding of Upton. Smarter than everyone and a master of putting us all down, my arrogant Renaissance man was propelled not by brilliance but by fear. He may have thought drinking protected him, and made him bold, but it only masked an aggressive anxiety.

Buff stayed through the summer and into the fall, getting sporadic temporary computer jobs through an agency. When he wasn't working, he helped with the children and the garden. We jointly coached Natty and Alex's soccer team, and during the day, when Upton was at work, I loved Buff's company. Sometimes he would go to Boston, he said to look for a job, and then not come home for a day or two. He'd look different when he returned, secretive and wasted.

After one of these jaunts I just said it: "Buff, where were you? Off at the baths again?"

He looked as though I'd slapped him. "How did you know?"

I think he meant how did I know he was gay, not how did I know about the baths, and all I really knew about the baths was that was where gay men met. I said I'd known forever that he was gay. So what? It didn't matter. This was monumental for Buff. He couldn't believe, first, that I'd known he was gay and, second, that it didn't matter to me, that it didn't change a single thing. We never talked about it again, I never said anything to Buff about Upton and Edward, and I never said anything to Upton about my moment of truth with Buff.

Upton and Buff were very uneasy with each other anyway, and as soon as Upton got home at night, they would both start drinking. Very soon, neither of them was good company. I would put the children to bed, serve up our dinner, and soon thereafter, go to bed myself, leaving them to spar in the living room, the bottle of Jim Beam uncapped on the sideboard. Upstairs, I would hear their voices, taunting, egging each other on. Sometimes there would be a crash, or the slam of a door. I thought back fifteen years to the old weekends when Lib and Buff and I were in New York and Upton would come up from Norfolk. There was drinking then, too, and I'm sure the seeds of anger and fear were already sprouting. But I was lost in the dancing, and in the promise of our shining futures.

At Christmas, everything came to a head. Oh, we did all the usual rituals: the tree, the candle, prayers, and Midnight Mass on Christmas Eve, Upton gathering everyone together Christmas morning with his "Hark! The Herald Angels"; we had presents; the fire was bright, the roast beef and Yorkshire pudding perfect. There were several fancy wines, and Upton had stocked the liquor cabinet with seasonal treats like port and cognac as well as the usual whiskies, vodka, and gin. Late Christmas afternoon, the neighbors; my parents; Upton's sister, Susie, the eldest of the Bradys, and her family; and my sister, Joan, and her family all dropped in for smoked pheasant, oysters, homemade pâté, and wild rice salad. Upton brought in the flaming Christmas pudding and everyone cheered.

When we finished doing the dishes, the children and I sprawled in the living room, drowsily going over the events of the day while the lights twinkled and the fire glowed. The dining room was raised three broad steps above the living room but otherwise completely open to it. This is where the liquor cabinet was, and Buff and Upton as well. They were ostensibly still putting bottles away and retrieving errant glasses, but their voices got louder, suddenly shifting from jocular to jeering and then, in an instant, to fury.

"When are you going to stop living off me, for Christ's sake?" Upton slammed his fist down on the table.

Buff didn't say anything.

"When are you going to stop guzzling my booze?"

Buff turned away, faced us in the living room, his face hard, eyes cold. I'd never seen him look this way before, as if he were fighting not to fight.

"Fucking freeloader!" Upton slammed the table again.

Buff turned back to Upton, still not replying, but I saw his shoulders stiffen, as if he were gathering himself, like an animal.

"When are you going to get a job? A life?" Upton moved closer to Buff, backing him into the liquor cabinet.

"I've got a job in January."

"What a liar!" Upton took a swing, Buff intercepted it, hung on to Upton's arm, and soon they were wrestling, like enemies, not brothers. I must have yelled at them to stop, I don't know. I do know I was in tears, and I know the children were, too. Buff, the athlete, was bigger, stronger, and not quite as drunk as Upton. He had two kidneys. He soon pinned Upton to the floor, kept him there, panting for a few long minutes, and then let him go. Upton staggered to his feet and fell, stumbled up again and fell. He barked out a laugh that sounded first mean and then pitiful, and began to crawl on all fours across the room toward the kitchen, while his children watched and wept. Upton, the drunken bully who had so often terrified me, was now on his knees, broken.

I started to kneel beside him as I would an injured child when Andrew jumped up, his soft boy's face still tearful but suddenly as full of fury as Upton's had been a few minutes earlier. He lunged up the steps toward his crawling father. I was afraid he would attack Upton, and I think Andrew was afraid he might, too. He paused, brimming with rage, injustice, all the potent emotions of a thirteen-year-old son for his father. Andrew stared down at Upton for a moment, turned away fast, and burst out the door into the freezing night.

"Andrew!" I shouted, running after him. "Come back!"

He turned and waved but kept on running across the snowy lawn. "I can't. Don't worry, Mom. I'll call."

He knew I couldn't leave the others, and I knew he would be all right. But I couldn't believe that Upton had driven his own son to run away from home on Christmas night. I went back in, to the beautiful tree and the crackling fire and the frightened children. Upton, still on all fours, wasn't going anywhere, his head now resting on the carpet. Buff leaned on the liquor cabinet, his head in his hands. Sarah held Natty in one arm, Alex in the other.

"Upton, get up. Come to bed." I tried to help him to his feet, but he was a dead weight.

"Why? Why should I go to bed?" he slurred.

"Because you are drunk." I heard an edge to my voice. "And you," I said to Buff, "you can help get him upstairs."

Together, Buff and I got Upton to the threshold of our bedroom door. I had stepped back to let Upton pass when, in a surge of energy, he wheeled around and faced me. The hall was narrow, and my back was close to the top of the very steep back stairs that plunged straight down to the kitchen. I didn't see his hand coming, and when it hit my cheek, I stumbled backward. Upton's hands were on my shoulders. And then he pushed. Buff caught me. I hung on to the railing while adrenaline flooded my body. As soon as I could speak, I told Buff to put Upton to bed. Still shaken, I went back downstairs to the children. Alex came running to me.

"Mom, I don't want to sleep here." Two weeks earlier he had turned nine, but Alex was small and right now, fragile-looking. "I want to sleep at Aunt Daisy and Uncle Gil's." Daisy and Gil were our neighbors, a mile down the road.

How could this be happening? This was Christmas night, the stage still perfectly set for celebrating the birth of the Prince of Peace, dispeller of darkness, source of infinite love. My cheek stung from my husband's hand; one son had bolted from the house, and another was too frightened to sleep in his own bed. My fourteen-year-old daughter was mothering her young brothers, holding back her own tears to comfort them.

Soon it was quiet upstairs, both Upton and Buff passed out on their beds. Andrew called from the Denny's restaurant four miles away, which was closing for the night. I left Natty and Alex with Sarah and picked up Andrew, standing alone in front of a dark Denny's, snow swirling in the wind.

"I'm sorry I ran out like that, Mom," he said, before he'd even closed the car door. "I shouldn't have left you. But I thought I might kill him."

The next day, amazingly, Upton and Buff were up bright and early, no sign of a hangover. In the sunny kitchen, they rustled up coffee, scrambled eggs, and cooked bacon while the Mormon Tabernacle Choir caroled from the stereo, as if today were just another day-after-Christmas, as if the drunken violence of the night before had never happened. Unthinkable! Look at this happy family, this perfect Christmas house. But every time I looked up at the perilous back stairs I knew it had. And I knew it would happen again. Yet I stalled, wanting to believe this morning sham of the happy family. Should I confront him alone or with everyone there? Could I wait until tomorrow? I mulled over the options, while the clock ticked ever closer to noon, the magic hour when the sun would be over the yardarm at last, and Upton would pour himself a drink.

"We have to talk." I watched the children freeze as if we were playing red light, the living room unnaturally silent. "In front of the children."

Finally Upton looked up from the *Times* crossword puzzle. "About?"

If it weren't for that tinge of frost in his voice I might have been persuaded that he truly did believe nothing had happened. I might have ended the conversation right there. Oh, how easy it would have been.

"About last night." I took a breath. "About your drinking."

"Sally, it was Christmas!" There was the nasty patronizing tone. "As usual, you squeezed in too much. I was *tired*." He gave me an arrogant, blue-eyed stare.

"No. You were drunk. You were a mess. You hit me."

He did not acknowledge hitting me, or trying to push me down the stairs. He did not apologize. He did not even react, except for his steady stare, so cold it felt like fire. I waited as long as I could stand it before filling the hostile pause.

"I can't go on like this. You are a drunk and you need help."

"I am not a drunk! I only drink because . . ." And here followed a long and tedious litany of blame. He drank because dinner was late; because after putting up with Peter Davison all day, he came home to chaos; because Buff was mooching off him; because no one paid attention to him—on and on, always returning to the same protest: "I am *not* an alcoholic!" According to Upton, he only drank because other people drove him to it. He could stop anytime he wanted to.

"Like today?" I asked.

He slapped the paper down on the arm of his chair and stood up. "It's a holiday weekend, for Christ's sake!"

"Does that mean you have to have a martini for lunch?" My heart pounded as I posed each question, expecting him to burst with anger. Maybe to hit me again, although I didn't really think Upton would do that if he were sober. And he was still sober.

"Sally, I don't '*have to have*' a martini for lunch. I *enjoy* having a martini for lunch. If you don't want me to, I won't." Again, that patronizing, singsong lilt.

"Good," I said, thinking that actually it wasn't so good for him to tie all this to me. But at least today he wouldn't get drunk at lunch.

"And, we need to talk to someone. A therapist." I wished my voice were more assured. I wished I were more assured.

"Why?" He said this like a challenge.

I could feel myself begin to buckle. No, I wouldn't weaken. Not this time. "Because we need help."

" 'We'?"

"I need help, Upton. I can't handle this alone."

Upton gave me an overly patient look, as if I were a needy child.

"It is certainly clear you need help," said Upton.

Aha! Maybe Upton would agree to go if I made it sound as

though he were doing it for me, which, in a way, he was. If I could just make him think that I was the needy one. As long as he wasn't to blame, then he might come along.

"Thanks," I said, watching as he brought his cigarette to his lips. "It will make a huge difference to have you there."

A family therapist had just opened an office in Bedford. I knew nothing about him except that he was nearby, and I called him on Monday. From the start, Upton resisted therapy, and unfortunately this jargon-spouting therapist only reinforced Upton's scorn. From the first meeting, Upton talked circles around him, beat him at his own game. We saw him once a week, and even brought the children for a visit. He was a caricature of a therapist, and I started to make fun of him, too. Desperate as I was for a safe place to bring my troubles and my husband, it didn't take long to know that this wasn't it. By Easter, we had stopped going.

Meanwhile, the tiny cottage very close to our house had unexpectedly become vacant, and the family offered it rent free to Buff until they found a permanent tenant. Getting Buff out of the house brought Upton some relief, though I would miss Buff. Not his constant presence, but his protection, drunken though it might be. Buff did get a job, too, just as he'd said he would. With Buff gone, Upton was on a mission to prove that unlike Buff, he was not an alcoholic. He would test himself by not drinking for a week. Then the next week, he would drink only wine and beer, because "they don't count." For a month or so he would only drink on the weekends, really fun for the family. But our lives had marginally improved, and we soldiered on.

Then Buff disappeared. Vanished, leaving an empty house, and leaving in a car he'd borrowed from friends of ours. For over a month, no one knew where he was, or what he'd done with the car. He ended up in Washington, D.C., bingeing on sex, alcohol, and drugs. I don't know who finally rescued him, or helped to rehabilitate him. I knew only that Buff had bottomed out, and was reborn into AA and a lifetime of sobriety. He joined a gay AA group in New York and turned his life around. Oh, and he also got the car back to its owners. Upton did not talk about any of this, and he didn't like it when I did. I believe the new, clean, openly gay Buff disturbed Upton even more than the closeted, addicted Buff; and certainly more than Lucy, who as a priest had to be discreet about her lesbian life. Lucy was also a recovering alcoholic. Three of the six Bradys were alcoholics; Buff and Lucy were gay. And Upton? Yes, he had had drunken sex with Edward. But that didn't mean he was gay. Did it?

Upton kept on playing with his drinking, still trying to prove he wasn't an alcoholic and still getting drunk. I tried not to think about the slap on my face Christmas night, or his hands on my shoulders pushing me backward toward the stairs. Besides, there were many other constellations in our household besides Upton.

Sarah was away at Northfield Mount Hermon School, where she'd been given a generous scholarship for her last two years of high school. She had researched private schools herself the year before, filled out the applications, and made appointments for interviews. Sarah had always been a good student, and if she were admitted to a good, private school, with a scholarship, I was sure she would benefit. I missed her company, and I missed her help with the boys. I also worried about her, about drinking, drugs, and sex and no parental supervision. However, I was glad Sarah was spared Upton's outbursts.

Andrew, so smart and so unhappy at Bedford High, was getting into fights, had no good friends, and had horrible grades. He ran away from home for ten days that fall, to the Cape, where he'd spent the summer with my parents and at last had made a few good friends. He'd left a heartbreaking note on the kitchen table: *"Dear Mom and Pa, I'm running away. It isn't you, it's school. I'll let you know where I am. Don't worry. I'll be okay. Love, Andrew. P.S. I'm taking the green blanket, I hope you don't mind."* I told the high school that it was all right with us for Andrew to miss a few weeks of school. He needed to get away, and I hoped he might go back to school and make it through the year if he didn't feel so locked in. Next fall, I would find another school for Andrew.

One morning at breakfast, when Alex was ten and already a veteran dancer with two *Nutcrackers* behind him, the two older boys were acting tough.

"You faggot!"

"Fuckin' fag!"

And so forth.

Upton was standing in the kitchen, gulping black coffee. He had to have heard them, but he didn't respond. After a few minutes, Alex piped up in his shrill little boy's voice.

"Listen, you guys don't even know what a faggot is. You've never even met one." All eyes were suddenly on the youngest child; the kitchen was his. "Well, every day I change my clothes with fags. They're just people. They're just like you and me."

I looked at Upton, hoping he had heard this truth from his young son. But Upton was already on his way out of the kitchen.

It was 1978, when probably more than half the men in the Boston Ballet were gay. Alex and I talked about it from time to time. He knew that gay men liked men, not women, and he seemed to know which dancers were straight and which were not. When the company was performing, he said the straight guys kept an eye on him, saved him a place in the dressing room, joked around with him.

One night shortly after eleven, Alex scampered out the stage door after a performance of *Sleeping Beauty,* eyes wide.

"Mom, you won't believe what happened to Arnold Frank tonight!"

Arnold was dignified, older, openly gay, but not one of the dancers who usually paid attention to the children.

Alex rattled on. "He forgot to remove his nipple ring before he went onstage and it got tangled up in his costume. When he took off his velvet jacket in the wings he was all bloody and his nipple was just hanging."

Now, what kind of parent lets her ten-year-old son stay up until midnight on a school night, dancing with men who wear nipple rings? When I told Upton about this, all he did was shrug, as if it were an insignificant detail. He never told me how he felt about Alex spending so much time in a gay culture. He only talked with great pride about Alex's talent and hard work; nothing about the ballet scene itself.

When we went to Alex's opening night as Fritz in *The Nutcracker,* Upton was stunned. All 3,600 seats in Boston's Wang Center were sold out. The house lights dimmed, and Upton took my hand, held it tight as if he needed courage. The orchestra played the overture, and when the curtain went up, there was Alex-as-Fritz alone onstage, asleep in a chair. Clara skipped in and the show began. Afterward Upton asked Alex in great awe how he could do that, be alone on that huge stage in front of all those people.

"Weren't you terrified?" asked Upton.

"Pa," said Alex, calm as an old hoofer, "don't you understand? Those people paid to see me. They are my friends."

Upton repeated this story the rest of his life, never losing a bit of his wonder and admiration for that small, sure son.

I had taken the ideal part-time job for a writer, three days a week, ten to three, answering a phone that hardly rang and keeping a calendar of lunch dates and club meetings for a retired real-estate appraiser. My hours in the airy, empty office on Beacon Hill gave me a little money, which I needed now that I'd stopped the day care, and a clear space to work on my new book, for which I had a contract. The writing was hard; the book stalled over and over again. I went day by precarious day, watching Upton's drinking increase, and wondered what I would do the next time he lost control. I didn't have to wait long.

On a rainy Sunday in April 1980, Upton got blind drunk at lunch. I was cleaning up the dining room with Natty, almost thirteen. We were rushing, as I had to pick Alex up in Boston after a rehearsal for *Sleeping Beauty*. I don't remember why Upton had flown into this particular rage, just that he had backed me into a corner and I was sure he was about to hurt me.

I turned to Natty. "Go! Go outside right now." I didn't want him to see Upton abuse me. But Upton had other plans.

He turned on Natty. "You stay right there. I want you to watch this."

Upton grabbed a kitchen chair and slammed it into the wall over my head. The chair itself missed my head, but the pieces broke all over me, scaring me, not harming me. Seconds later, Natty and I stood amid the wreckage in a kind of vacuum, watching Upton slowly crumble. He didn't fall down, he just slumped against the door, vacant, as if he'd been knocked out. I don't think he ever knew exactly what he'd done. He knew something terrible had happened. He knew he was drunk. But nothing else.

"Upton, you have to leave." How could my voice be so calm? "You can't stay here. Get some clothes and get out."

"But where will I go?" He was weeping, lost in his own house.

"I don't know. Go to a motel." I fished in my wallet and gave him two twenties, enough for several nights at a motel and suppers at McDonald's. "I have to pick up Alex. When I get home, I want you out."

Natty came with me to Boston. We collected Alex at the theater, and I tried to tell the boys that we would work this out, that it would be all right. I could tell that Natty was worried, not about us but about Upton. And so was I. When we got home, there was a note from Upton, his handwriting shaky, the letters unevenly formed. I had never seen him write like that. *"Gone to Travelodge. Love, U."* I called my good friend Morgan. He had watched Upton's drinking affect us all over the years, and he knew how worried I was. He had also told me about his own wonderful shrink, who was connected to Harvard Medical School. I needed to find a first-class therapist, right away. Today. In a few hours, Morgan called back, and minutes later, I had an appointment with a psychiatric social worker, Catherine Morrison, for the very next day. I gathered up the broken pieces of chair, put them in the woodstove, and struck a match. Anything to relieve the chill.

That night in our bed, where Upton's scent still lingered, I thought of the weeks when he'd been in the hospital two years ago and I'd slept with his pillow under my head, praying for him to recover, to come back to us. During those weeks without him, our lives had seemed unanchored, the air around us dead. Life without Upton was gray. This afternoon, I had made him leave. Now that vibrant element was gone. I thought of him, twenty-two years old and in tears, taking me in his arms on Second Beach, the first time he said he couldn't live without me. He'd said it many times since then. Maybe it was true.

When I found out about Edward, I chose to stay with Upton, not out of need or duty, but because I loved him, loved his company, loved what he brought to me of his world. All this was still true. Except now I wasn't sure I could live with him any longer. I wasn't sure it was safe. I thought of him alone, in the shabby motel room. Did he know what he had done or where he was headed? Did he know how much I loved him?

VERMONT, JULY 2008

I am home from New York, my hair has never looked better, and I'm getting ready to spend a week on the Vineyard with Natty and Tracy and their two small boys. The first morning I was in New York I had breakfast with Marcy, a writer Upton had worked with as a freelance editor after he left the Atlantic. They had never met over the three or four years they'd worked together but had a lively correspondence and an even livelier telephone exchange. Often when Marcy called I would answer the phone, and we, too, struck up an odd, long-distance friendship. She hadn't been in touch for several years and didn't know Upton had died until a few days before our breakfast.

I felt an instant kinship as Marcy and I quickly fell into stories about Upton and ourselves. I had left Vermont feeling so unsure of Upton's love for me and so full of doubt about the true nature of my marriage. Finding the gay porn had eroded my belief that in spite of everything, Upton had truly loved me. I now wondered if from the start he'd thought of me more as his rescuer than as his lover, and sitting across from Marcy in the Four Seasons as Upton's widow, I felt like a fraud. Marcy has a vibrant and direct honesty.

"You know how Upton adored you," she said.

He did? How does she know this? She never even met him.

"He used to talk about you when I called to go over the book." She then went on to tell me what he'd said, little things, like what I'd made for supper, or grown in my garden, or published. Random bits of praise.

"He was so proud of you—I could hear it in his voice."

My eyes filled and I couldn't reply, which was lucky, because if I had, I surely would have spilled the truth about my doubts. I did tell her, when I could speak again, that her words couldn't have come at a more crucial moment. They were salve on an open wound. Maybe my doubts were wrong. Maybe I was not seeing the whole of my life with Upton, in its true color and proportion.

That same day, I had a late lunch with Jim, another of Upton's writers. Jim and Upton had met many times, but Jim and I had not. We hadn't even spoken on the phone until after Upton's death. I knew he was a businessman and wrote historical novels full of war and religion. He was cordial and easy, but I didn't feel that intimate spark I shared with Marcy. We ordered, talked about his book. And then he looked at me and took a breath.

"I'm so sorry about Upton. He used to talk about you all the time."

Upton had spoken of me to Jim? This was a surprise. Upton, so private, so circumspect about what he said to people, especially with men. I was stunned that Jim knew more than my name.

"He told me about your workshops, and your own writing. It sounded like an amazing partnership." He looked away. "You must miss him terribly."

Within four hours, two strangers had affirmed Upton's love for me, just when I most doubted it.

Now, back in the house where he lived and died, I try to sort out the conflicting truths that have surfaced since March. There is the life he shared with me, his love, his life partner. And the other life, with glistening strangers. I go into the upstairs bathroom, where he died. I study the tub. I do this frequently, seeing Upton the way I found him that night, trying to imagine how it was that he could fit in that narrow porcelain space as he had. Last month, I even asked Alex to climb into the bathtub to see if he could replicate Upton's position. Now I climb in myself. It's awkward and uncomfortable. I get back out, staring at the emptiness and without thinking, I say again what I'd said that night when I leaned over him, stroking his smooth, clammy cheek, his still damp hair.

"Good-bye, my love."

They say that hearing is the last of the senses to go.

Sally and Upton.
Tarpaulin Cove, Naushon Island, Massachusetts, 1984.

PHOTOGRAPHS BY MORGAN MEAD

7

All sorrows can be borne if you put them into a story.

—ISAK DINESEN

VERMONT, AUGUST 2008

Last November, for our forty-fifth anniversary, Upton produced an elegantly wrapped box. I could tell by his eager look as I unwrapped it that he was pleased with this present. It was a cassette, *The Best of the Everly Brothers.* I was certainly surprised—we hadn't mentioned or listened to the Everly Brothers in years, and while it brought back all sorts of memories, I'm afraid I wasn't nearly as thrilled as Upton expected me to be.

"Aren't you going to play it?"

Most of our music is now on CDs, and he'd forgotten that our cassette player didn't work. But I still had a tape deck in my car, and the next day, that's where I listened to the Everly Brothers. I'd forgotten how great some of the songs were, and how close their harmonies. I played it a couple of times, and then brought it in to my study, where I kept my cassettes.

A few days later, Upton wanted to know if I'd listened to it.

"I did. It brought back the old days," I said. He waited, as if I had more to say. "Thank you!" I said, again.

"Would you mind if I borrowed your car and listened to it?" he asked.

"Help yourself!"

A few days later, he gave it back, and it sat in my office for four months. Then, a couple of weeks before he died last March, he came to me with a worried look.

"Where's that Everly Brothers tape?"

"I think it's in my study," I said, feeling a little guilty because I hadn't played it in a while.

"Are you sure?"

"Pretty sure."

"Well, don't lose it."

Why was he making such a fuss? Was I missing something? A few days later, he brought it up again.

"Did you find that Everly Brothers tape?"

"No, but I will. You want to borrow it?"

He shook his head. "I just want to make sure you have it."

I've thought about playing the tape many times in the six months since Upton died. I keep thinking I should look for it, but I don't, afraid that maybe it isn't in my study after all, maybe I've lost it, and I just can't face that. Yet today, for some reason, I just march in and open the cassette box, and there it is. I am hugely relieved and carry it to the car. But I don't play it. Not today. Maybe tomorrow? For over a month now, the tape has been in my car, unplayed. I don't know what it is about it that makes me wary, any more than I know what Upton found so important. Another mystery to solve, I guess.

Today I am on my way to see Catherine Morrison, our former therapist. I knew she had moved to Rhode Island when she retired four years ago, and last week I called her, hoping she might tell me things she knows about Upton that I don't. One thing I am still so desperate to understand is where Upton kept his homosexual self, his longings and fears and joys. I wonder if there were any joys in that compartment. I wonder if there even was a compartment. I hope Catherine can fill in some of the gaps. She was shocked and very sad to hear Upton had died. The three of us worked for six years together, and then she and Upton continued on for another twenty more. Even after we moved to Vermont, Upton continued to drive to Boston to see her. On the phone, she sounded as eager to see me as I am to see her.

I want to find out if she knew that Upton continued to sneak alcohol, or that he had finally stopped smoking, less than a year before he died; I want to see if she knew about his debt. It's almost a four-hour drive to Tiverton from Vermont. I think about Upton as I so often do in the car, a safe place when I can cry if I want to. I see the Everly Brothers tape on the shelf and put it in, thinking it's weirdly appropriate to finally do this on the way to our therapist.

I wish Upton and I had listened to it together. We could have taken a spin last November seventeenth in my red Toyota, rollicking down the hill, listening to the same tunes we'd heard in the solid-gold Pontiac forty-five years ago. Now I am heavy with regret.

I put on side A: "Bye Bye Love"; "Wake Up Little Susie"; "All I Have to Do Is Dream"; "Bird Dog"—all the big hits. But I hear nothing that makes me think of Upton. Now side B: "Claudette"; "('Til) I Kissed You"; "Poor Jenny"—definitely all side B tunes. Maybe I should give up trying to find something from

Upton in an Everly Brothers song. The next one starts, and suddenly the words fill the air in my lungs. "I bless the day I found
you . . ." A physical reaction akin to fear sweeps through me and
I pull over to the side of the road, my eyes streaming. I feel almost sick. "Without your sweet love, what would life be?" This,
this is what Upton wanted to tell me: *let it be me.*

I push rewind and play it again and again, all of the verses,
each word resonating, pulsing through me. Of course this
would be how he'd tell me. Upton was the king of quotes. He had
always relied on other people's words to express his deepest
feelings—brilliant quotes from the Psalms, Shakespeare, Milton,
Homer. Oh, and Kipling, of course. He used other people's
stories, too, from the New Testament or Greek mythology or
from someone's own life, like Edward Weeks's. And he used other
people's songs—Gilbert and Sullivan, Harry Belafonte, the Everly
Brothers. Upton took on these words and turned them into his
own language for expressing feelings. The words he knew by
heart were sturdy, proven rafts to carry him across the swirling
sea of emotion. *Now and forever. Let it be me.*

BEDFORD, 1980–1996

The day after Upton broke the chair over my head, I had my first appointment with Catherine Morrison. When Morgan had asked his doctor to recommend a therapist for Upton and me, he said we needed someone who was wise and accessible and had a sense of humor. I knew before my first hour with Catherine was up that she fit the bill, but maybe what drew me to her the most was her compassion. As a psychiatric social worker rather than simply a therapist, Catherine was skilled at solving daily problems, such as how I should go about safely letting Upton move back into the house from the Travelodge. She told me to insist that Upton agree to the following:

Number one, he was not to get drunk or abusive. She didn't say he had to stop drinking, which was wise. Upton had always ridiculed therapy, and the months with the creepy counselor a year ago had made him even more critical. I was afraid he wouldn't meet with Catherine at all, and if he did, the trick would be to play him like a fish and keep him coming. If part of the deal was to stop drinking, it would never work.

Number two, he must commit to therapy. I would see Catherine alone once a week; Upton would see Catherine alone once a week. And we would see Catherine together once a week.

"You tell him he must agree to come twice a week, and to not get drunk or abusive." She looked at me with great kindness and great severity. She was giving me an order.

I thought of saying this to Upton. It was terrifying. "I can't. I can't possibly tell him that."

"Why not?"

"Because he will get furious."

She put both her hands on my shoulders and looked me in the eye. "You don't understand," she said in her gentle North Carolina lilt. "Upton is already so furious that nothing, absolutely nothing you do, can possibly make him any madder."

Could this be true?

She nodded. "Believe me, whatever you say, it won't make any difference."

With those few words, Catherine removed a crippling weight. It was like magic. Nothing I did would make Upton any angrier. I was free.

Upton didn't like the conditions of his homecoming, but he did agree to them. He was very uncomfortable at our first meeting together with Catherine, and brought up all sorts of reasons why he couldn't commit to two hours each week. Catherine calmly unraveled his objections, and our meetings began.

I looked forward to my private hour with her every week. She showed me how to distinguish my part in the recurring impasses and flare-ups with Upton. I always knew that nothing was ever all his fault or all mine, but I wasn't practiced at spotting what I could change in myself to keep from getting sucked into Upton's loop, or into my mother's. Sometimes I brought up my mother and Upton in the same breath. Week by week, I would tell Catherine how shamed and powerless I felt when they wrongly accused and misjudged me. With Catherine's help, I learned to spot old habits, and eventually to discard them. I saw myself in a new light. I saw Upton and my mother in the same new light. We were all separate.

The weekly appointments with Upton were different and difficult. What I valued the most about our meetings together was that Catherine provided a safe place for each of us to say what had happened since we last met with her. Upton's and my views of any simple exchange between us were almost always fraught. Upton skated just above his river of rage, and often the ice was paper-thin. He would burst out of the room, scrambling for the cigarettes in his pocket, and Catherine and I would hear the front door slam. A few minutes later he'd be back, carrying echoes of rage and whiffs of smoke.

After the first month, Upton wrote Catherine a careful, articulate letter, suggesting that writing letters replace meeting face-to-face. He believed that for him, therapy-by-mail would be far more effective. This was so like Upton, it made me both laugh and roll my eyes when Catherine brought it up, telling him gently but firmly that she didn't think this was a good idea at all. I waited for Upton to object. To say something like "Well, if that's the case, I won't be coming anymore." But the stakes were high, and he continued to come. He also continued to drink. He didn't get roaring drunk, at least not when he was with me, and he never raised his hand to me again.

This was a turbulent time in my own therapy with Catherine. I was learning so much, and yet Upton remained stuck, unable to handle his anger, unable to surrender his single point of view. The more aware of myself I became, the more aware I was that Upton really did not know who I was. He had invented another Sally, on whom he superimposed his own needs and fears. Catherine showed me the depth and complexity of Upton's pathology, and it was hard not to despair. For him to really change, he would have to address the issues that made him drink in the first place, and to do that, he would have to stop drinking.

I began to talk with Catherine about leaving Upton. I didn't want to do it, felt guilty even thinking it, but I was lonely and I was sad. When I think of this time in my life, I think of myself as always being on the brink of tears, if not awash in them; of being ashamed of my weakness and desperate to keep the tears hidden. Sometimes I slept in the spare bedroom. Several times I woke myself up in the middle of the night with a great, frightening cry erupting from deep within me, a cry so strong that it made my throat hurt. I stopped wearing my wedding ring for several months, hoping Upton would notice and ask me why. He didn't. I wondered what my life and the children's would be like if Upton and I separated, and what Upton's life would be like without all of us. I thought he would probably suffer the most. Catherine promised she would tell me if she thought that there was no hope and that I should leave him. I trusted her, and I also asked her more than once if she thought the time had come.

"Not yet," she'd say, with great compassion. "And besides, you still have work to do."

She was right. The work had been hard and steady, but my bruises were still fresh, the rips and rents of separation not yet completely healed. I had become my own person, yes. And when Upton accused me falsely of ridiculous offenses, I might no longer take the blame, but I still felt an immense sorrow and sometimes anger, too, that he still saw me as the villain, the dark power, the one who made his life such a misery. Worst of all, there was nothing I could do to change his views.

I went through periods of writing down his accusations:

"You are incapable of *ever* serving dinner on time!"

And the reality:

"Monday, Feb. 2: dinner at 6:58; Tues., Feb. 3: dinner 7:01; Wed., . . . etc."

But I soon saw that my obsessive records were, in their way, just as crazy as Upton's accusations. I knew what time I put dinner on the table, and very gradually over many weeks, I came to see that Upton might well go through the rest of his life always and forever feeling that dinner was late, no matter what time he picked up his fork.

In February 1982 we had a disturbing meeting with Catherine. I mentioned something I had seen on Upton's desk. I can't remember what it was; not Upton's journal or a private letter, but a shared communication—an invitation to a party or something like that. I had picked it up, read it, and returned it to Upton's blotter. He was livid. His desk, handed down through generations of Uptons, is known as the Upton Desk. It was built in the eighteenth century for Upton Scott and designed after Chippendale. It requires a lot of space, both vertical and horizontal, and the only place we had room for it was in the dining room, a thoroughfare between the living room and the kitchen. Everyone passed by the Upton Desk all the time, and I don't think it ever occurred to us that we shouldn't touch anything on it, although Upton had never actually said so. Yet I think we all respected that it was his desk. None of us would ever think of sitting at his desk, or rooting around in the drawers. I was astonished that he was so angry. We spent that hour with Catherine solely on my breach of privacy, and ended with my promising Upton that I would never, ever, touch anything on his desk again.

A few mornings later, Upton drove off to work at seven-fifteen as usual, the school bus spirited the children away a few minutes later, and I tidied up and got ready to meet my sister, who was coming from Providence to take me to lunch. At ten-thirty the telephone rang. It was Upton, sounding weak and disoriented.

"What's wrong?" I heard clatter in the distance. He wasn't calling from work. "Where are you?"

"Howard Johnson's. The Fresh Pond rotary." He was close to tears. "I couldn't get out of the rotary; I just kept going around and around. I couldn't stop."

"Shall I come pick you up?" I didn't understand anything except that Upton was in trouble.

"No. Just call the Atlantic. Tell them I'm sick. I'm coming home."

Call the Atlantic. I did, thinking how like Upton to make sure he let them know. Then I thought about what must have happened. Upton would have gotten to the rotary by at least eight. Had he been driving in circles for two and a half hours? When he got back home he was pale and shaken. He didn't want to talk, he wanted to go to bed.

"Do you know what happened to you?" I wondered if I should call a doctor, or Catherine.

He shook his head. "I couldn't stop circling. I couldn't stop."

He climbed into bed, ashen, shaking, fever-free but drenched with fear.

By this time, it was too late to tell my sister not to come. Maybe it would be good to give Upton some room, some peace. I left with Joan, telling her Upton wasn't feeling well. When I came back at two, his car was gone. My first thought was that he had killed himself. I looked on the kitchen table, where we usually left notes, but there was nothing. I went past his desk on the way to the front door and saw an envelope in the middle of the clear blotter: SALLY. I reached for it, and stopped. Less than a week ago I had promised to never, ever touch anything on Upton's desk. And now here was a letter from him to me. Desperate, I called Catherine and spilled out the whole story.

"What shall I do?"

"Open the letter!"
"But—"
"Don't be ridiculous, open it."

> Dear Sally,
>   I am checking myself into Emerson Hospital. Don't worry.
>   Love,
>   Upton

Upton spent six weeks on the psychiatric floor of Emerson, the first two heavily dosed with Valium to help him through severe alcohol withdrawal. As soon as he was able, the hospital escorted him to daily AA meetings and set up psychiatric counseling as well. Upton hated AA, hated listening to everyone's stories, hated the idea of having to tell his own story, the real story with all its warts and hangnails, which I don't think he ever did tell to anyone.

The sixth week in the hospital, he went back to work but continued to live at Emerson. That Monday morning on his way to the Atlantic, he stopped at St. Paul Church in Cambridge, where he had worshipped when he was at Harvard, and where we continued to go as a family. Weekday mornings at eight, the Mass is run by the boys in the choir school and is a kind of choir practice for the coming Sunday. For the next six years, Upton went to morning Mass on his way to work. He said this was his AA, and I believe it was. He also went to the hospital's own therapist-run weekly meetings for people with drug and alcohol problems, people who, like Upton, didn't want to go to AA. Upton didn't find these meetings very helpful and stopped going after a few months. But he stayed sober and never missed an appointment with Catherine or Mass at St. Paul's.

In many respects, the next ten years were halcyon years, even though the new, sober Upton was quite different from the mercurial wonder-worker I had married. He no longer moved in the swirl of bright energy that had drawn people to its light. Upton was quiet, often removed. He no longer wanted a social life, especially at night. He was tired. Therapy with Catherine was hard work and often led us through bad patches. She gave us exercises to do together that encouraged us to be more open and trusting. She told us to leave the unresolved issues and discord outside the bedroom door, which wasn't as hard as it sounded. One of my sorrows when Upton was drinking had been the loss of physical intimacy. Sober, he worked hard to restore this. He read books on sex and became a superb lover. But even so, sex with Upton was rarely spontaneous. He said he'd like to reserve Saturday nights for what he impishly called "a party." He surprised me with candles for the bedroom, fragrant oils, and pleasurable new techniques.

He found inventive ways for us to take cheap weekend trips using frequent flier miles for hotels in Boston or Newport or Nantucket. We spent our twentieth wedding anniversary at the Trapp Family Lodge in Vermont, two free nights in return for listening to a forty-five-minute pitch for a time-share. In addition to the Saturday night date, we had a standing date for dinner out, every Friday, no children, just the two of us, a way to formally put the workweek behind us and mark the beginning of the weekend. He never wanted to celebrate the end of the week by making love. That was reserved for Saturday. Each Sunday night, to close the weekend, we ordered pizza and watched

Masterpiece Theatre. I enjoyed our weekend routine, but every now and then it felt prescribed and I would long for passionate spontaneity and whimsy.

Catherine had studied with Dr. Herbert Benson at Beth Israel Hospital in Boston and believed that mindful meditation might be helpful to Upton in resolving some of his anxiety and anger. At first he balked, but Catherine persisted. At the same time, he had begun to suffer from tremendously painful attacks of gout. After he lost his kidney, Upton developed hypertension, for which he was taking Dyazide, and the Dyazide brought on gout. There had been a rash of articles and books claiming that meditation could lower one's blood pressure. Upton began to meditate every morning, for his blood pressure, he told us. In a very short time, his blood pressure dropped and he stopped taking Dyazide. And, as Catherine had hoped, meditation also brought insight and peace. Yes, in many respects, these were halcyon days.

Yet in spite of weekly therapy with Catherine, Upton still couldn't emerge from what Catherine explained to me was a narcissistic personality disorder, something she said didn't even have a name until 1980. I immediately thought of Narcissus falling in love with his reflection, but this was not how Catherine defined clinical narcissism, a condition that usually indicates a very fragile self-esteem and vulnerability to criticism. She emphasized how difficult it was to treat, and explained that narcissists often lose the ability to empathize with others. So Upton truly couldn't see me as I really am. Instead, said Catherine, he conjured up someone else, someone who shared many of his mother's problems, and many of his own. No matter how hard I tried to reveal myself to him, he couldn't help seeing his own hybrid version: I was needy, dependent, weak. This after I had found an excellent therapist, written a successfully published novel and a number of pieces for mainstream magazines, and managed four children who had very different interests and needs, and for the past few years, our finances.

He was so off the mark it was almost laughable. But I didn't laugh, because to Upton, I still wasn't really there. He was married to someone else.

Catherine pointed out that the elements he'd ascribed to me were the elements in his own life that he hated.

"This," she said, "is a classic example of the kind of transference we call mirroring."

I began to understand.

She also explained that what narcissists fear most is abandonment. If I believed I was incompetent and needed him to survive, I would never leave him.

"You always expect *me* to pull *your* chestnuts out of the fire!" Upton would say, completely fed up. Or "Why are you so needy?" Or "As usual, Sally-the-victim!"

"Now, Upton," Catherine would instruct in her mild voice, "take the witch's hat off Sally." And from time to time she would remind me, in private, that narcissism is never easily resolved.

Of course, I didn't ask Upton what he and Catherine talked about privately. Sometimes he would volunteer a new insight, or give me Catherine's interpretation of something he or I had said or done. I knew he was working hard, and I was relieved that finally Upton had someone he could trust with whom to share the things he held so tightly to himself. I wondered, too, what Catherine knew of Upton that I didn't. Probably volumes.

TIVERTON, RHODE ISLAND, AUGUST 2008

The first thing I do when I get to Catherine's is tell her about the tape, sing her the song, my voice catching on "so never leave me lonely." Then I tell her about Upton's last year, his last day, and how he'd said he wanted to return as a stone. We briefly talk about the solid, unchanging nature of stones, and of their safety.

"He never was able to talk about emotions easily, was he?" I say. "Not even with all those years of therapy."

Catherine shakes her head, as sad as I.

"Emotions were quicksand to him." A rueful little laugh escapes as I speak. "Sometimes I think he married me because I wallow in enough emotion for us both."

Catherine agrees.

"Not that Upton wasn't emotional," I rattle on. "He was. He just couldn't let it out." I think about this for a minute, and then add, "He couldn't let his emotions out because it was too dangerous." I take a deep breath. "Like being gay."

Silence.

I look at Catherine, waiting for her to agree.

She is speechless. Maybe because she didn't know that Upton had shared his secret about Edward with me, and that's why she seems shocked.

"I mean, being gay for Upton must have been the worst possible sentence, don't you think?" I ask her.

Finally, Catherine replies. "Upton was gay?"

Now I am the one struck nearly dumb. "You didn't know?"

She shakes her head, still stunned.

I tell her about finding the pornography; I tell her about Edward.

Catherine, his wise and trusted therapist for over twenty years, did not know anything about Upton's homosexual side. I say "side" because I still do not know what Upton was. Can you be a little bit gay or is it like being a little bit pregnant? If you are bisexual, does that mean you enjoy sex equally with men and women? Then there is MSM, which I've only just learned about: Men Who Have Sex with Men. Apparently, this does not mean the men are gay. I wish I understood this but I don't.

I look at Catherine, still in shock. How could this never have come up in all those years of therapy? Perhaps this is the key. It never came up because Upton didn't bring it with him to Catherine's office. He left his homosexual self in a separate locker somewhere, a little like the way Catherine had encouraged us to leave our marital baggage on the other side of the bedroom door. I run this past Catherine, but she shakes her head, more in disbelief than disagreement, and still looks baffled.

Before I leave, Catherine and I agree to keep on meeting whenever we can.

"Upton loved you, you know that," she says as we stand at the door.

"I do know that," I say. And I do. Upton's love for me was deep and lasting.

What I do not know, and what troubles me more every day, is whether Upton truly knew in his heart, in his very bones, how much I loved him. Before I know I've done it, I blurt this out to Catherine, standing there in the open doorway. I finally say it out loud. "Did he know, do you think he knew, how much I loved him?"

She looks at me, her face very sad, and slowly shakes her head. "I doubt it."

On the way back to Vermont, I try to get beyond this. Catherine and I both know how hard it was for Upton to love himself; how impossible, then, to know how we loved him. This is really the great tragedy. Not a new tragedy; nor a fleeting one.

I think about how Catherine did not know Upton as well as I. Yes, she and Upton had worked to uncover old childhood traumas, damage severe enough to lead to a lifetime of self-medication. And because of Catherine, Upton had made significant changes. But how could she not have known about the rest? We have Upton the publisher, the straight married man, the homophobic Catholic with the writer wife and four fine children, the recovering alcoholic with childhood scars. This is the Upton who balked at counseling until he saw how it helped him understand himself. This is the Upton who worked so hard for almost thirty years to change, the Upton Catherine knew so well.

And then we have Upton the furtive homosexual, the drunk, the sneak, the liar. This is the Upton who started drinking and smoking while he was still a child, probably, I think now, to ease the pain of homosexuality. Catherine never met the gay Upton. Like the trash bag outside the bedroom door, this Upton never crossed Catherine's threshold.

But my speculation is flawed. I don't really think there were two Uptons. It's just that this is as far as I can get right now. The Upton I loved said he couldn't live without me, and I think he was right. Without me, he could not have lived in the light-filled, moral, and accepted straight world. Without me, he could not have gone to Mass, or faced his mother. Without me, he might not have found Catherine, or the part of himself she helped him discover. *Without your sweet love, what would life be?*

I play the song over and over again on the long drive to Vermont, my free hand on the empty seat beside me, my face wet. *Always let it be me.*

8

Intuition assembles information that the mind has learned and forgotten, arriving at a conclusion that appears to come out of nowhere.

—DONALD HALL

CAMBRIDGE AND WOODS HOLE, NOVEMBER 2008

On November 1, All Saints Day, I have lunch with Morgan. Morgan is a writer, a teacher, a great favorite with my children and with me. And he is openly gay. I haven't seen him to talk with since before Upton died, and I tell him the whole story: the debt, the porn, Catherine's not knowing. When I am done, Morgan takes a deep breath.

"I am going to tell you two very important things. First, it is common for supposedly straight and married family men to have gay sex. I know. These guys have come on to me. It happens all the time."

This is news, something I'd never guessed before. I quickly think of Edward, and wonder for the first time who seduced whom.

"Second," Morgan continues, "it has nothing to do with you."

"How can you say it has nothing to do with me? It has every-thing to do with me!"

"I meant it doesn't mean Upton didn't love you."

I feel as though we are back at square one. Doesn't anyone get it? Upton had a secret life. He betrayed me when he had sex with men. Of course it had to do with me; it was huge.

Morgan isn't finished. "Listen," he says. "You've got to please tell your story. It will help a lot of people."

So I do, and the story pours out; details fly, one after another in a blizzard of separate moments I never expected to relive. I get up before sunrise to write in bed; I fall asleep with the chro-nology of my marriage trying to reassemble itself. The children know I'm writing this—they've even read the first half. They want more.

"This must be a good catharsis for you," said Andrew, and although he said it kindly, there was something patronizing in his tone that made me want to wring his neck.

This is no catharsis! I look it up in the dictionary to make sure. *"Catharsis: the process of bringing to the surface repressed emotions, complexes, and feelings in an effort to identify and relieve them, or the result of this process."* Right. The emotions that fire through me are not repressed. Haven't been repressed. They are current, oh, that is the truth. Some of them are like an electrical current. And they have been skimming across the sur-face of my consciousness throughout my marriage—throughout my life. Any buried or repressed emotions were pretty well flushed out in the therapy with Catherine. We swept those cup-boards clean.

It's not hard to identify my emotions. What's hard is filling in the gaps of a forty-six-year love affair. How will I ever know if

Upton truly loved me? If he wanted to remain in the marriage? If secretly, he longed to leave? I think about ransacking his files for journals, letters, anything that might tell me who he really was. I open one, the last one, see some notes about drinking, and put it away. I don't even go through my own journals. Instead, I go back to the safety of my own flawed memory. I will only write about what I think I know. What's hard is to meet the secrets, hold them in my hand, run my fingers over the contours, and find the right place to put them in this puzzle of missing pieces. But I worry that I'm losing the knack of seeing the puzzle as a whole, of seeing it in that singular way so necessary in order to recognize how each piece fits. I'm too close.

And besides, I have a million questions for Upton, my toughest and best critic. His edits were always sharp; not only that, they made me laugh, even when they were bad-tempered. When he read my schmaltzy essays and short stories for the ladies' magazines, he'd say, "Congratulations! This is at least a three-hanky story." If it had to do with Christmas he might even give it a four-hanky rating.

When I wrote my novel, he gave me the title, *Instar,* a single, potent word that refers to the weakened, vulnerable state of a crustacean just after it sheds its shell. It is a great word, one he discovered while working on William Warner's Pulitzer Prize–winning book *Beautiful Swimmers,* about the blue claw crab.

There was the Friday before the long Memorial Day weekend when my editor at *Woman's Day* called, desperate for a Christmas story.

"Can you do it over the weekend?" asked my editor. "Fax it Tuesday morning?"

And I'd said yes.

That night, over Scrabble, Upton knew I was panicked.

"Okay," he said, "let's make a list of all the elements we can think of that might go into a Christmas story. Like candles and stars, and the possibility of angels."

"Stop! That's it! *The Possibility of Angels*! That's the title. Now all I have to do is write the story." And I did.

Well, so far, I think Upton would call this one at least a four-hanky story. And I hope it would bring him relief, not shame.

The big question will never be answered, though.

"Do you mind if I tell this story?"

NEW YORK AND BEDFORD, 1986–1996

Labor Day, 1986, and the house was emptied, Sarah off to Connecticut College, her duffel lumpy with art supplies, Andrew to Boston with chef's knives and guitars, Natty to Colorado shouldering skis and fishing rods, and Alex and Upton to New York, Alex to his shared apartment near the School of American Ballet and Upton to his spanking-new studio near Penn Station.

The preceding winter, Carl Navarre had bought the Atlantic Monthly Press from Mort Zuckerman and decided to move the offices from Boston to New York. Most of the old Atlantic Monthly Press staff left the company, Harry Evans, the director, to become founding editor of *Condé Nast Traveler*. Upton, still executive editor, agreed to move to New York, and we began our two-year commuter marriage. Upton still met with Catherine in Brookline every Monday morning, before he hopped on the train to New York, and sometimes I went, too.

Like Miss Newlywed, we joked, he was obsessed with finding the right pied-à-terre, which turned out to be a roomy bed-sitter in the old Hotel McAlpin on Thirty-fourth Street and Sixth Avenue. Then he was consumed with furnishing it. He found the perfect bed/couch arrangement—two beds with drawers beneath and fat, wedge-shaped bolsters above, plus end tables and headboards with shelves. Put in an "L," this became a comfortable and attractive living-room unit. It also came with a cheap chest of drawers and a drop-leaf desk with shelves. Best of all, Macy's called it a Teen Fantasy Set, and so did we. Upton bought a dozen assorted pillows, a new rug, a complete set of Revere Ware pots and pans, china, glasses and stainless flatware for eight plus place mats and napkins for his new teak table. He drew a floor plan of the apartment so I'd have an idea what it looked like, and then he made paper cutouts of each piece of furniture, which we moved around for days to determine where everything would go. I hadn't seen Upton as enthralled with a project in years. He seemed young again, in a swirl of infectious optimism.

The six years of intense therapy had worn me out even as they had given me a growing understanding of myself and my own predictable tangles with Upton and my mother. My meetings with Catherine had tapered off, and I only met with her when Upton and I hit a specific snag. I had loved my times with Catherine and used to think that if she weren't my therapist, she might be one of my best friends. But I was sick of talking about the same old tangles with Upton and besides, I was enjoying a curious new freedom from both his and my mother's manipulative ways.

No longer afraid of their reactions, I could openly disagree with each of them, sometimes teasing Upton and shocking myself and the children with an edge of sarcasm that sneaked into my voice. Most of all, I enjoyed a spaciousness I'd never had before. I put away my old, flawed novel and wrote more personal essays and short stories for *House Beautiful, Woman's Day,* and similar publications.

When Upton announced he was moving to New York, Alex was thrilled.

"Pa, we can get an apartment together!"

"Are you crazy?" said Upton, sounding horrified but clearly pleased. "Don't eighteen-year-olds want to get away from their fathers?"

"I'd like to live with you—bacon for breakfast! A nice, clean apartment with real furniture, not a messy pad."

"Whatever makes you think that *I* want to live with a teenager?"

Oh Upton, how could you be so hard on your generous son? But Alex just laughed. "Yeah, I'm pretty messy."

I thought of Upton's Ninety-second Street apartment twenty-five years ago, and the pride and pleasure he'd taken in it. In the years since then, he had barely tolerated the confusion of a house full of children, animals, guests, other people, me. He never liked adjusting his routine to accommodate someone else and especially loathed it when people kept him waiting, as I often did. So he and Alex had their separate apartments, Alex and roommates in a certain amount of adolescent disorder and Upton in his own reliable space where no one ever moved a paper clip or threw out yesterday's crossword puzzle. He often cooked dinner for Alex, and he had two extra sets of keys made, one for his wife and one for his son.

"The apartment is yours, Alex. On weekends or whenever I'm not here."

For Upton, this was a giant step.

One rainy October weekend, when Upton was in Germany at the Frankfurt Book Fair, Morgan came out to Bedford to visit. He brought with him Nigel Nicolson's riveting chronicle of his parents' unconventional union, *Portrait of a Marriage*. We spent the weekend reading the entire book aloud to each other in between feeding children and drying wet socks. Harold Nicolson and Vita Sackville-West were well-known British intellectuals, each with homosexual lovers, and their affairs were not always discreet. But the marriage itself was solid and nurturing. They enjoyed each other's company, produced two sons whom they adored, wrote books, designed gardens, and were literary lights.

I envied the Nicolsons their marriage and brought up the book and Morgan's visit the next time Upton, Catherine, and I all met together. When I'd finished telling them about this rich and singular marriage, neither of them said anything right away. Catherine looked puzzled, as if she didn't quite know why I'd brought it up.

And then Upton burst out, "I don't know why you think they had such a great marriage!"

"They were close, they loved each other, they shared their lives, even though they had lovers, even though they were gay."

"They were perverted. Like Morgan. Why do you always hang out with fags?"

"Would you rather I hung out with single straight men?"

That was the end of that conversation, at least as far as Upton was concerned.

I waited for Catherine to say something, but she kept silent. I hadn't brought up homosexuals before. And now it was almost as if I never had.

A few months later, Upton came home from New York for the weekend with the terrible news that Buff had been diagnosed with AIDS. In a joint session with Catherine that Monday morning, I brought it up. Before she could respond, Upton broke in.

"Serves him right!"

His words filled the office and then lingered like a vapor of fratricide while Catherine and I searched for something to say besides "*Upton!*"

A few weeks later, we were at Catherine's for another early Monday morning appointment together, just settling into our usual places, when I blurted out something I never knew had ever crossed my mind. I had no idea where it came from, perhaps from some buried layer of intuition. Like an earthquake or an exploding gas line, the words seared through my mouth.

"We should agree to tell each other if we have sex with anyone else," I said, aghast at this declaration. I was certainly not planning to have sex with anyone else. Catherine seemed surprised, too. But Upton was frozen, a statue cast in bronze.

"Well?" I prodded. The words were out. "Do you agree?"

"Why do you ask?"

"Because of Buff, I guess. Because of AIDS."

Upton shrugged. "I see."

"So you agree?"

"Whatever you say."

"Is that a yes?"

"Will you stop haranguing me!"

He never actually said yes, though I pretended he had.

These were the only times homosexuality or AIDS ever came up when we were both with Catherine.

I went to New York every now and then for lovely weekends during which Upton was not just my husband but also a gracious host. There would be fresh flowers on the table, and delicacies for dinner from the Union Square farmers' market or Dean and Deluca, which Upton would cook for me. We would play Scrabble, just as we did after dinner in Bedford, with Mozart or Haydn or maybe a Chopin nocturne in the background. We would make love on one of the narrow beds of the Teen Fantasy Set, and sleep apart.

On November 17, 1987, Upton and I celebrated our twenty-fifth wedding anniversary, appropriately in New York. Before we left for dinner and dancing in the Oak Room at the Plaza,

Upton opened a split of champagne for me and poured himself a goblet of Perrier. Then he took from his pocket a small domed velvet box, similar to the one he'd given me at the Carlyle in November 1962. Inside was a ring—not an ordinary ring, but something Upton had put together on his own, without my knowing, from stones I already had.

In 1959, before I really knew Upton, my closest childhood friend, Samm, gave me a luminous emerald-cut aquamarine from Brazil. It had lain in my jewelry box ever since, waiting for me to have it set. I wanted to have it flanked by two smaller stones—something pale and yellowish like peridot. In the late seventies, I showed the aquamarine to our friend Jacques, who traveled often to Africa and returned with his pockets full of semiprecious stones. A few months later, two small triangular citrines the perfect size and pale color to augment the aquamarine appeared on the kitchen table. Now there were three unset stones in the bottom of my jewelry box. I imagined the finished ring with the aquamarine standing tall, citrines like little buttresses on either side, but when I showed the stones to my old boarding school roommate, Bonnie, who has an eye for design, she quickly turned the aquamarine on its side, to lie horizontally between the citrines. Neither Upton nor I would ever have thought of this, and it made all the difference.

Now here it was, the three loose stones, gifts from people I loved, set in Bonnie's design and all put together by my Best Beloved, without my ever having had a whiff of his surprise. I slipped the ring on above my wedding ring, where the little cabochon emerald engagement ring used to sit until it got too tight to slide easily over my knuckles. The ring was like liquid in the sun. Right away, people were drawn to it. Strangers eyed it across the room, friends touched it with their fingertip or even held out their hand, waiting for me to slip it off for a second. My ring was not costly; the semiprecious stones were gifts; the gold setting perfect but not showy. Later that night, Upton and I waltzed in the dusky Oak Room, our bodies together in their old close fit, the length of my legs against his, our feet fast and sure on the parquet floor. I looked from the ring, flashing as we turned, to my clear-eyed husband, now five years sober.

The Atlantic Monthly Press fell on hard times when it moved to New York. Carl Navarre first sold the children's imprint, which had long sustained the company during lean years, and then went on to sell its illustrious backlist. Upton left after two years, returning to Bedford in the summer of 1988 with his Teen Fantasy Set, new pots and pans, and a golden handshake from the Atlantic. I didn't see any of this windfall directly, though I was pleased when Upton traded in our one Subaru for two Le Cars, and happy with the fine Oriental rugs he found on sale. He bought new clothes, corduroys and Viyella shirts instead of tailored suits with vests from J. Press (or J. Squeeze, as he used to say when the bill came in).

Mostly, Upton used his six-figure check to live on, and allowed himself the summer to begin his own novel. I was still piecing together enough work from writing workshops at Harvard, freelance editing, and writing for the slicks to pay my half of our living expenses. Upton steadfastly kept to his old Atlantic schedule, getting in his early-morning walk, breakfast (when he stopped drinking, he started eating breakfast—scrambled eggs and toast and bacon, every day), meditation. By nine-thirty, Monday through Friday, Upton was at his desk. He would go out to lunch at twelve-thirty sharp, returning by two for a short nap, and then stay at his desk until six. As I flitted back and forth to Cambridge, stole an hour or two to weed the garden, had breakfast at eleven and lunch at three, meeting writers in between, I both envied and resented Upton's unwavering schedule.

Soon after he got home in July, Upton declared a vacation week. Monday dawned, beautifully sunny, and off we went to Crane Beach. The beach wasn't crowded, and I decided to walk its four-mile length while Upton napped on his towel. Beyond the last lifeguard's chair, there was only a mere scattering of people. The barrier dunes that run the length of the beach are high and almost a quarter mile deep in places. On an empty stretch of beach, high on a dune, I spotted a lone male, facing the beach. As I got closer, I saw that he was naked and I hurried on. A little later, I saw another man, also naked. And another. When I got back to our towels, I told Upton about this phenomenon.

He raised his eyebrows as if I were making it up, looked disgusted, and headed for the water. That was that.

The rest of the summer was hot, and almost every Saturday and Sunday Upton and I would head for the beach. Without children in tow, our outings were different. We no longer trekked all the way to Plum Island but to Crane, with its huge parking lot, showers and changing rooms. We would leave home later, and stay at the beach until the shadows lengthened. Then we'd shower and dress for dinner, stopping at a bistro we liked in Ipswich, overlooking the river. On several scorching weekdays when I had commitments, Upton would decide he'd had enough writing, grab his neatly packed beach bag, and head for Crane on his own. I applauded this spur-of-the-moment deviation from his prescribed workday.

When we went to Tarpaulin Cove for our usual two weeks

around Labor Day, I began to suspect that Upton was drinking. I never actually saw him drink, but he was often garrulous, silly. I also sensed him physically shrink away from me sometimes, as if he didn't want me to touch him. I knew I should confront him, but I didn't want him to lie to me on the one hand, or confirm my fears. Finally, on the beach, the Scrabble board between us, I simply said that I would leave the Cove if he kept on drinking.

"What makes you think I'm drinking?"

"The way you smell, the way you talk too much. Did you really think I wouldn't notice?"

He didn't drink again at the Cove, and I didn't leave.

When we got home, Upton gave me the first sixty pages of his novel to read.

"I want you to give me your honest opinion," he said. "The way I did with your book. Don't be kind."

"Okay." Our eyes met.

"Listen, I've had a lot of fun writing it. I'm not expecting it to really fly."

Which was fortunate. What he'd written was certainly literate; it was funny (except that I'd heard most of those lines many times before); it was clever—a little too clever, perhaps; and it didn't work. The characters were broad, predictable, and too familiar; the plot was obscure. Upton knew all this. He took the verdict with grace and some relief, I think, and told me he'd really like to start a literary agency.

"We could do it together, partners with separate writers. Brady Literary Management."

In the fourteen years of my writers' workshops, I had occasionally given an outstanding manuscript written by a student to Upton or other editors I knew, acting as an unofficial agent.

And with Upton no longer at the Atlantic, some of his authors now were delighted to reattach themselves to Upton in a slightly different way. Brady Literary Management seemed like a natural segue for both of us. With new writers flooding in, the space in my life formerly occupied by the children was full to bursting.

But as my life expanded, Upton's suddenly shrank. He had no place to go, no colleagues, no office away from the house, no assistant to answer his phone, no lunch dates. And no friends of his own, something I think is true for many men. He did have writers, some from his Atlantic years and some new referrals. However, unlike me, Upton kept the people he worked with quite separate from his personal life. He groaned when people invited us to lunch or dinner or for weekends on the Vineyard. But he knew I would accept. And he seemed to enjoy himself at parties, though he'd never admit it.

Once a week, he saw Catherine. While he was more aware of his anger, he still was not always adept at handling it. He could often recognize his black-and-white view of the world but continued to have trouble admitting that his point of view was not absolute; that his way of cooking bacon, for instance, was not the only way or the best way to cook bacon.

In public, Upton drank only sparkling water, but he never did stop drinking. I knew he took a swig from the brandy bottle when he deglazed the steak pan—I think he especially enjoyed doing it when I was in the room, turning his back so I wouldn't see, like a rebellious adolescent. When I went away, Upton would drink. It's all in his journals, in messy, drunken penmanship.

"Drunk again! I feel like shit!"

Once I found an empty pint bottle of vodka in the waste-basket, still in its brown paper bag. That time I did confront him.

"I wish you wouldn't drink when I go away."

Upton gives me a chilly look. "What makes you think I drink?"

I hold back the evidence and force the lie. "Didn't you?"

"Of course not. I've stopped drinking. You know that."

Now I produce the bottle in the bag.

He looks whipped.

Later he apologizes for not telling the truth.

"You know how to tell if a drunk is lying?" he says, with a repentant gleam in his eyes.

I shake my head.

"Are his lips moving?"

In 1993, after almost fifty years of smoking, Upton decided to stop, go cold turkey. We were at the Cove, and he intentionally did not bring any cigarettes. Overnight, he went from two packs a day to no cigarettes at all and immediately plunged into a gripping depression that didn't let go for almost three years, even though he started smoking again almost immediately. He could barely get up in the morning, but he did, locked into his routine of morning walk, meditation, work, nap, etc., which may have been what led him through his days. None of the myriad wonder drugs his psychopharmacologist prescribed brought him any relief; in fact, most of them produced terrible side effects—nausea, diarrhea, hives, headaches, in addition to the depression. And they made Upton impotent. Compared to the depression itself and the other side effects of the drugs, impotence seemed inconsequential. Except that sex could have been an occasional source of comfort for us both, a way to bring Upton back from the terrible isolation of his depression.

When we moved to Vermont in 1996, Upton found a new psychopharmacologist who was determined to discover a mixture of meds that would lift his depression without the crippling side effects. It took nine months to find the magic potion. We both noticed a change beginning in December. Upton seemed to be climbing back into the light, slowly, rung by rung. We hardly dared speak of it. Then, at Midnight Mass on Christmas Eve, surrounded by flickering candles, evergreens, and resplendent vestments, we heard the familiar words from the Epistle:

"The people that walked in darkness have seen a great light: they that dwell in the land of the shadow of death, upon them hath the light shined."

Upton reached for my hand, a surprise, and held it tight. I turned, and saw his face, streaming with tears.

"I never really knew what those words meant until tonight."

There was only one, small side effect that came from this perfect mix of Ritalin, lithium, and desipramine: Upton's continuing impotence.

Here he was, sober at last, and finally free from depression, and yet still impotent. How unfair. But Upton seemed relieved. Sex with him was no longer an option, and something he expected me to accept. But I didn't.

"Sally," he said more than once in a tired voice, "we're *old*."

"Upton"—I tried to sound pleasant—"fifty-six is not old. Nor is fifty-seven."

I asked him if he thought he could do something about this, and he got a prescription for Viagra. I thought at the time that he did this more for me than for himself. The Viagra helped, but the mechanics were still difficult. There was something pathetic about the whole attempt, as if we were doing this to be kind but not for fun or for passion or even for relief, and finally we just gave up.

More puzzling to me, and so difficult, was that Upton shied away from any spontaneous physical touch at all. Planned, routine, physical contact—holding hands every morning, the kiss of peace at Mass, farewell and welcome home embraces, these were all fine. But a squeeze in passing, a kiss on the cheek, a quick neck rub—all these old welcome touches from Upton vanished. I continued to touch him the way close friends and lovers do, off and on throughout the day. These were not preludes to making love, they were just a continuation of the friendly physical affection we'd always had. But at least since his depression, or maybe even before, when I touched Upton, I felt something different: the tiniest flicker of a flinch, almost imperceptible but for a slight stiffening in his neck and shoulders, a distance in his eyes.

"Why do you flinch?" I'd blurt this out only rarely, not sure I really wanted to know the answer.

But Upton never gave me an answer. "Flinch?" he'd say. "What do you mean, flinch?" Or "I have no idea what you mean." Or he would simply not react at all, as if I had never spoken.

In November 1999 Andrew and Mari were married in Atami, Japan, and Sarah, Natty, Upton, and I all spent a week in Japan. The only bilingual person in either family was Andrew, and judging from the expressions of those he spoke to in Japanese, his language skills were not as refined as they might have been.

The morning of the wedding, Andrew appeared at our door, holding out a white shirt. "Could you iron this?"

Upton plugged in his little travel iron, fashioned an ironing board out of a futon, and seated on the tatami mat, ironed Andrew's wedding shirt. When he finished, he got up and gently pulled Andrew close, making the sign of the cross on his forehead. A father's Christian blessing for his firstborn son before the Shinto marriage ceremony.

A month later, we welcomed the new millennium the way we welcomed each new year, with vicious backgammon for ten cents a point, and a final reckoning of the year's running total. At midnight, we stood in the open doorway, arms around each other, breathing in the cold, clear air of the twenty-first century.

One day in January, I answered the phone and it was Nikos! He and I had never been completely out of touch, though there had been long intervals of absence. His first marriage, to a Greek woman, was brief. He published two books, and a few years later met Clare, a vivid young Englishwoman whom he eventually married. The last time our paths had crossed was in 1983, when Alex was dancing in Connecticut not far from where they lived. He and I spent a night with Nikos, Clare, and their baby. Five years later, Clare died, leaving Nikos, at age fifty-two, the single parent of a six-year-old child.

My pulse quickened when I heard his familiar, sonorous voice. Nikos was calling because he had finished another book, this one a curious combination of memoir and adventure, and he wondered if I would read it, with an eye toward becoming his literary agent. Of course I said yes, and a few weeks later we met in New York. His beard was gray, his brow more noble, but his eyes still smoldered. He handed me a brown shopping bag with his manuscript, and when I got back to my room, I started to read.

Nikos went back to his childhood. He writes with grace and a wry wit, and reading his words was like hearing him tell me his story out loud. I read on, through the years of prep school and his first year at Harvard. And then, suddenly, there I was on the page. He had changed my name to Eternal Beloved, and when I read those words, the tears started. I am but one part of his story, as he is but one part of mine. But in both accounts, our relationship is important and lasting.

While he was rewriting the book, we saw each other fairly often. There were frequent e-mails and phone calls, and when I went to New York, we would meet. Upton knew I was working with Nikos, and seeing him in New York and sometimes in Cambridge. In the months that Nikos and I worked together, a flurry of what-ifs began to blow past: What if the old spark could be reignited? What if we could have an old-fashioned fling? What if the old spark turned into a blaze? Oh, how I would love to be swept off my feet again. And what would I do if it happened?

In May, Nikos invited me to drive with him to Montreal for the weekend, saying he'd always wanted to travel with me. When I told Upton about the invitation, he knit his brow, and pulled out his calendar. "May . . . what?"

I repeated the date.

"I'm not sure I can commit to that right now." He flipped through his date book.

"That's okay, Upton," I said, gently. "You weren't invited."

"Oh." He closed his date book.

"I hope you don't mind if I go?"

"Not at all—have fun!"

We had an easy and companionable drive north, Nikos and I, but he wasn't happy with the hotel. We soon found another, where he booked a suite with two separate bedrooms, each with its own bath, and a small, private hall connecting the rooms. We swam, each had a massage (my masseuse referred several times to my "husband," which gave me a frisson), napped separately, had a late dinner together, and retired to our own rooms. Very peaceful. The next day after breakfast in my room, we walked the city, he sketched, I wrote, we ate. It was companionable. I wondered what it would be like to live with him. There was a reserve, a mystery, and such a possibility seemed distant. In the afternoon, we visited some friends of his, an older couple who gave me a warm welcome. But on the way home something changed. Nikos seemed uneasy, almost sick. The cab back to the hotel had a strong, cloying deodorizer swinging from the visor. Suddenly Nikos turned to me.

"Your perfume!" he said. "It's making me sick!"

"I'm not wearing perfume." But he didn't seem to hear me, and by then we were at the hotel.

Dinner that night was a little stilted, and we left the next morning, chaste as siblings. Something had shifted.

Hungry as I was for someone to love me, court me, bed me, dissolve all boundaries for a brief time, would I have ever left Upton for Nikos, or for any lover? No. I like to think that I could have given in to a glorious passion, but I'm not at all sure I could have done even that, and alas, I never really had the chance.

Seven years later, Upton suddenly lost his words over Sunday lunch. First it was two words, then more and more until within fifteen minutes, every sentence had holes. Upton was losing what he loved most. He looked at me, incredulous, yet with a sweetness that startled me. He looked like a young child, wide-eyed as his toddler grandson. Words had always been Upton's luster, the wings for his agile knowledge to take flight. I wanted to whisk him off to the hospital, but he was adamant about staying put, taking his nap, which he was sure would restore his verbal skills.

When he woke up, he had retrieved a few words, except that when he used them, they weren't the right ones. He pretended it was nothing, but now I could see fear in his blue eyes. The next day, Monday, he insisted on driving to the post office to pick up the mail, and driving again to lunch, as usual. I tried to persuade him to stay home, but Upton had his routine. He worked on the mindless crossword puzzle in the local paper, and folded the crossword page open in *The New York Times*. But even the Jumble in the *Valley News* was too much. That night, I looked at the blank squares, rubbed thin and gray with erasures. Monday was the worst; on Tuesday, he filled more than half the squares in the *Valley News* crossword, and he finished the Jumble. But all the squares in the *New York Times* puzzles remained perfectly empty. On Wednesday, I announced that we were going to the ER. Tests confirmed that he had suffered a transient ischemic attack (TIA). The important word here is *transient,* and by Friday, Upton had all his words back. Talking to him, you would not have guessed what had happened.

"I don't know what you're carrying on about! It was nothing."

Or "I was simply tired!"

But starting that Sunday, what scared me more than the thought of Upton dying was the thought of Upton living without his words. For him, I think, they were tangible proof of everything he valued most—history, facts, intellectual superiority—and the only safe way to express emotion. Words were how he chose to communicate. Without his words, Upton's suffering would have been unbearable. I never asked him if he would rather die than live in a verbal desert, but had I done so, I think he would have preferred death.

Two weeks after the first TIA, Upton had a second one, this time when he was swimming at my sister's. He spent three quiet days in the hospital, with all his words but very little energy or eagerness to resume his old life. When I visited him twice a day, he seemed pleased to see me but undemanding— no requests for pencils, books, clean underwear. *The New York Times* from the day before lay uncracked on his table. He didn't mention going home. He was removed yet peaceful, as if perhaps he was turning toward a future he knew would be brief.

Upton's last days of summer and first weeks of fall were filled with doctors' appointments, tests, and a battery of new prescriptions. Only sixty-nine, he became an old man almost overnight, fragile as translucent china. Worrisome thoughts about our future popped up everywhere. I grew alert to ordinary lapses of his attention when he drove or shopped, or made supper. I often checked his progress with the *New York Times* crossword puzzles, and held my breath when it looked like he might miss a standard move in backgammon. He seemed frail, but very much himself, intellectually sharp; just a quieter Upton. He hated all the fuss and all the pills, but he seemed less worried. I think we both took a deep breath as the tensions that had built since July began to ebb.

Early in November, I was cutting back the peonies and mulching the beds for the winter when I realized that I was doing this lying down. The clippers felt unusually heavy in my hand, and I was hot. When I stood up, I lurched, suddenly dizzy. Feverish; a victim of an unidentified virus and one that was resistant to even the newest and most costly antibiotics. For four weeks, Upton nursed me through fevers of 103 degrees, total fatigue, and weakness. We missed the big family Thanksgiving at my sister's and had a peaceful little local chicken, which Upton stuffed with wild rice. I drank Prosecco in my bathrobe and beat Upton at backgammon. I gave thanks for his loving care—for the pretty trays of consommé with toast points and endless clean sheets; for his good company.

In February, Alex came to visit. Upton told even more stories than usual, some bleak, revealing his many blackouts when the children were young. The stories of his own growing up in Portsmouth were brighter, especially the one about the summer he was twelve, when he saved the money he earned picking peaches to buy a matinee ticket to see Maria Tallchief dance at the Newport Casino. He rode his bike five miles each way to see her, returning forever smitten by Tallchief, by ballet. Alex and I wonder out loud if given the chance, Upton would have become a dancer.

"You have a dancer's body," said Alex admiringly. "And the perfect feet."

Upton's strong, wide feet with their Michelangelo arch were famous when Alex was a teenager. Whenever he brought home a new ballet dancer girlfriend ("bun heads," we called them), he'd ask Upton to show off his feet. Upton would take off his shoes and socks and the girls would ooh and aah. I'm not sure Upton had the temperament for ballet—I can't imagine him longing for criticism the way most dancers do. Would the discipline of ballet have been a comfort to him or a source of rebellion? Had he been a dancer in the fifties and sixties instead of a Harvard man and a naval officer, Upton might have been able to be openly gay. And yet I don't think that even as a dancer, he would have chosen that way of life.

Upton and Akira Upton Birnie Brady.
Tarpaulin Cove, Naushon Island, Massachusetts, August 2006.

PHOTOGRAPH BY MARI BRADY

9

Time does not bring relief; you all have lied
Who told me time would ease me of my pain!
I miss him in the weeping of the rain;
I want him at the shrinking of the tide.

—EDNA ST. VINCENT MILLAY

MARCH 2009

Right after Upton's death, Jem's generous wife, Marion, invited me to be her guest for a week's cruise on the *Norwegian Dawn*. She let me choose the dates, March 28 through April 4—a year and nine days after Upton died—and the route. I chose the Eastern Caribbean, because it included Saint Thomas. It's odd to think of visiting Saint Thomas without Upton; I always thought that someday we would make this trip together. We would swim in the turquoise waters of Magens Bay and lie on what Upton declared to be the most beautiful beach in the world. At night, we would dance the merengue at The Gate while the steel drums throbbed.

Now, on this still, early morning, the ship is gliding into Charlotte Amalie while I lean on the rail of our balcony, thinking of Upton standing on the bridge of the U.S.S. *Boxer* fifty years ago and seeing what I now see: the brilliant water that changes color over reefs and rocks; the steep hillsides covered with purplish-green vegetation; boats resting on their moorings, one wooden sloop that looks just right for Upton and me. An uninhabited island points south, and on it I see ruins of what looks like a fort. How many times did Upton, in his Navy whites, pass this island on his way ashore? How often did he visit this Garden of Eden?

Two weeks ago, I went to an anniversary Mass for Upton at St. Paul's, in Cambridge. I hadn't been to St. Paul's since he died, and I was unprepared for the terrible shock of missing him so acutely there, where we had lived so much of our spiritual lives. I knelt, thinking of all the eight o'clock weekday morning Masses Upton had celebrated here, and of the comfort and strength he'd found. At the kiss of peace, I was glad I was sitting in a sea of empty pews and could share my peace with the Upton I carried with me. *"Pax, soror,"* he used to say as he pulled me close, his lips brushing my cheek. I prayed for him, not for his life after death, but for the suffering in his life.

One long-ago Christmas Eve, when I was pregnant, I said that I wished I could pray for the Virgin Mary's labor pains, and Upton told me I could.

"Think of T. S. Eliot and the intersection of time with the timeless. It doesn't matter that Mary was in labor over two thousand years ago," said Upton. "There is no time in God."

Yesterday, the cruise ship had anchored off Samana, a peninsula on Santo Domingo. A small open boat had taken about twenty of us to a national park consisting of many tiny limestone islands, some with beautiful caves, once used as holy places, where a haunting spiritual presence lingers still. Our guides were kind young Samanans in bright blue shirts, white shorts, and bare feet. After exploring the caves on foot and the labyrinth of islands by kayak, we returned to the open boat to wait for an exchange of passengers. The radio was playing steel band music, and the Samanan crew moved with the beat as they tethered the kayaks and served up rum and Coke.

We were a motley group: three pretty high school girls with their parents, several retired couples, a few swinging singles. I was surprised when Louis, our shy, twenty-something guide, asked me, with my silver hair, to dance. Louis's body moved as he spoke, but he was the only one dancing. That didn't matter to me; I couldn't possibly say no to such an invitation. There was hardly any room, but all we needed was the little patch of warm deck beneath our feet and the music.

Dancing with Louis was not like dancing with Upton. For one thing, there was air between us. We were apart, yet we moved as one. I think Louis probably danced when he brushed his beautiful teeth and drove his car and sat in his classroom at the community college.

He bowed and smiled. "Madame, where did you learn to dance like this?"

"My husband," I said.

Louis's face glowed. "Ah! That explains it."

And it explained something to me, too. Upton had learned the merengue perfectly, and when he danced, that was the only thing he did. Louis, on the other hand, danced while he did everything.

When had I last danced with Upton? We danced at Sarah's wedding, in 1992, and I wanted to dance with him at Natty's wedding in 2005.

"Come on, Upton," I'd coaxed, reaching for his hand.

"I can't," he said, shaking his head. "I'm exhausted."

He *was* exhausted, that was true, from three rainy days cooped up in a borrowed house with his sister Lucy, crippled and in pain, and with Andrew and his darling, fractious two-year-old daughter. As we waited to proceed down the aisle, Upton had fingered the razor nick on his neck and lamented the dot of blood on the collar of his best wedding shirt. His back hurt.

"You dance." He squeezed my hand and with a sad smile, stiffly threaded his way among the dancers, going home to check on Lucy and tuck himself into bed. The evening had just begun. I danced with Natty, and with Alex. I danced with their friends whom I'd known for thirty years; I danced until late into the night. But I never did have that last dance with Upton.

By now the *Norwegian Dawn* has docked in Yacht Haven and Marion and I are in the van headed for Magens Bay, zooming around hairpin turns, plunging sharply down toward the blue water and white sand. From up high, the view is breathtaking. Upton was right—this is the beach of all beaches.

But when we reach sea level, there are acres of cars and a long line of open stalls offering bad fast food, suntan oil, T-shirts, drinks with parasols. The beach is so crowded we can't find a place to park our rented chairs, and the air is heavy with old French-fry grease, not frangipani. We are glad when our van reappears a few hours later.

I ask our white-whiskered driver if we are anywhere near The Gate.

He regards me with a slight frown on his smooth dark brow. "The Gate? Nowhere near."

"Can I get a taxi?"

"Why you want to go there?"

I sense his disapproval. Because I am almost seventy and alone?

"My husband used to go there," I tell him. "I want to see it."

He lights a cigarette and looks out at the harbor. "Not good place for you." He says this like a kindly father to his child.

Something tells me to drop it. I want to get back on the boat. I'm done with Saint Thomas. I hate the crowds of graceless tourists, pushing their way into the duty-free shops. I don't like Dronningens Gade, the glossy main street that masks the terrible poverty behind it. But there is something else I can't identify that makes me want to leave.

Back on the ship, I Google "Saint Thomas, 1959," and there it is: When Upton first came to Saint Thomas, capital of the Virgin Islands of the United States, it was one of the few places where men could be openly gay. I think of the faraway yet almost studied look on Upton's face when he danced. What was going on behind his distant blue eyes? What did he long for? I go back to the summer of 1989, when back from New York, he replaced his baggy Brooks Brothers bathing trunks with sexy, silky fig leaves, and took off alone for the beach. It never occurred to me that he might be meeting men in the dunes or that he was buying gay porn from Alex's friend Eric in Lexington. I still have so many questions.

MAY 2009

I keep hoping that I will hear from Upton, that he will come to me in a vivid dream, or that I will sense his presence beside me. But there has been nothing, even though I look for him every-where. The other day sparks flew from the socket when I turned on a lamp. I saw that the cord was badly frayed, and remembered how Upton used to repair such plugs. I would do it. It couldn't be all that hard. But it was, and I couldn't get it right. Maybe I should just replace the entire cord, from the inside. The lamp was china, a wedding present that, like most of our china lamps, had been knocked over by dogs' tails, toddlers, and wayward soc-cer balls and skillfully pieced back together by Upton. I turned the lamp upside down, and removed the old felt from its base. There was a piece of paper inside, faintly yellow with age. I fished it out, jolted by the familiar penmanship. "Help!" it said. "I'm be-ing held prisoner in a lamp factory!"

Oh, Upton, when did you write this? Who did you think might find it? Of course, tears are streaming down my face; of course I am laughing, too. I had almost forgotten his playfulness, his verbal spontaneity and whimsy. It wasn't the message I'd been looking for. Not one of them has been. But this one brings wel-come levity to the sea of unanswered questions.

Months ago, my friend Kitty gave me the name and tele-phone number of a gifted psychic in New Mexico.

"I think she might help," said Kitty. "Give her a call."

I start to place the call when the absurdity of consulting a psychic by phone and putting it on my Visa hits me. I could hear Upton saying, "Don't you think that's a bit woo-woo?"

And I don't make the call.

I have lunch with my friend Dan Jacobs, hoping that he, as a psychoanalyst and someone who knew both Upton and me socially, might clarify how Upton could have seen himself whole.

"How could he have worked so hard with Catherine, and never admitted his attraction to men?" I ask.

"Upton didn't repress his homosexuality; he kept it in another world." Dan looks sad. "He had two distinct and separate realities."

There it was. Not two Uptons, but two realities; two worlds that Upton must have struggled all his life to keep separate and secret from each other. I believe Upton saw one world as light: the visible world, the one he let us see. And there was his secret, shadow world. He and Catherine met in only one of them. But with me, they had collided—when he told me about Edward; perhaps sometimes when we made love, or didn't; and now, I am sure, when we danced the merengue.

I think of the exquisite beauty of Saint Thomas, ringed by an ultramarine sea, its steep hillsides dotted with pastel cottages. That is one Saint Thomas. Another has a shortage of potable water and hides its hungry children in rank shacks behind the crowded duty-free shops. And then there is Upton's Saint Thomas, where handsome men with liquid hips could dance together, leg to leg, at The Gate while the steel band pulsed. Suddenly, I see the truth. Upton never meant to bring me to Saint Thomas. Nor did he ever tell me that he wanted to. I had assumed he wanted to share his island with me, but all these years I have been wrong. This, for me, is a major piece of the puzzle.

And maybe it's enough. I look at old photos of Upton, and

of Buff, bright, shining boys. How did this happen? When did they first think they might be gay? Who were their first partners? Finally, I do it. I pick up the phone and call New Mexico.

I like the psychic. She sounds normal, intelligent, not really woo-woo at all. I give her some background information and settle in to listen while she records our hour-long session on a CD, which she will then send to me. She talks about the coming year, and how I will move through my grief and memories. She talks of my children, my elderly mother, my sister. She grows very concerned about someone I can't identify whose life is threatened. I don't know who this person is; she says he is on medication but that he will soon go off it and something very bad will happen to him in the next six weeks.

Then she asks if I have any questions.

"Yes," I say. "I really want to know about Upton's past. This is why I called you." She takes a breath, and then there is a long silence. I wonder if I've lost her. Then I hear her breathe again.

"In the past," she begins, "you and Upton were both Mongolian warriors."

Am I hearing this right? Maybe she is some kind of whacko after all.

"You were both men; both fierce leaders. And you were lovers."

I was on the edge of laughter, but now I am quiet. Rapt.

"In this society, homosexuality was accepted, and yet you and Upton, passionate lovers and faithful partners, chose to keep your relationship secret."

Secrets! Even in a former life.

"You came back as man and woman in order to have children."

This is making a crazy kind of sense.

"You are partners through eternity."

And that is the end of the call. I find it bizarre; and I also find it comforting. I think about it often. Sometimes I can't help giggling a little. I think someday I might even call her back, to see if there is more.

Then, two weeks after the phone call, a young relative, nineteen and bipolar, goes off his meds and kills himself, just as she had warned.

I could spend the rest of my life trying to understand Upton. But who among us can truly know what is in another's heart? What I know is that Upton chose me and that he loved me. I think that is enough.

It is now September, a year and a half since that snowy day in March, and I am in Atlanta for the opening of Alex's new show, Twyla Tharp's *Come Fly Away,* a dance musical with Frank Sinatra songs choreographed by Tharp for fifteen dancers. Alex, my baby, turns forty-one this year, and he can't dance forever. I've never missed an opening, but this is the first one I've been to alone. Upton would have loved this show, even though Alex's part onstage doesn't require much dancing. He is the MC, the gracious host, impeccable in a dinner jacket and a bow tie, with a new, well-trimmed beard and dignified bearing. He told me before the show that his bow tie is the kind that really ties.

"Like Pa used to wear," said Alex. "He's the one who showed me how to tie them. Every night when I put it on, I think of him."

The other dancers, in slippery, shimmering costumes that let us glimpse their strong, supple bodies, thrill the audience with emotional, dazzlingly difficult, and often acrobatic dancing, while Alex looks on, a pleased benefactor.

The turbulent second act begins to wind down. I expect it is about to gather itself together for a grand finale when the music suddenly slows and segues into Sinatra singing "My Way." The stage is dark and empty except for Alex. He is bathed in light, his bearing reflective, as if he were reviewing the whole evening, the full life he'd lived as he now faces the final curtain.

I never liked this song, and neither did Upton, but tonight the words catch me. *And more, much more than this, I did it my way.* Alex doesn't look like Upton, but right now, for me, he *is* Upton, surveying the empty stage with a familiar grace, remembering the riot of emotions that have so recently streamed across it, while he presided, safely upstage. Downstage now, and close to the edge, for just a moment, eight bars of four, he takes a few neat steps and jumps. Airborne in the light, my partner for eternity turns, opening his arms to all of us.